British History in Perspective
General Editor: Jeremy Black

PUBLISHED TITLES

Titles continued overleaf

List continued from previous page

Ann Williams *Kingship and Government in Pre-Conquest England*
John W. Young *Britain and European Unity, 1945–92*
Michael B. Young *Charles I*

FORTHCOMING

Walter L. Arnstein *Queen Victoria*
Ian Arthurson *Henry VII*
Toby Barnard *The Kingdom of Ireland, 1640–1740*
Eugenio Biagini *Gladstone*
Peter Catterall *The Labour Party, 1918–1945*
Gregory Claeys *The French Revolution Debate in Britain*
Pauline Croft *James I*
Eveline Cruickshanks *The Glorious Revolution*
John Davis *British Politics, 1885–1939*
David Dean *Parliament and Politics in Elizabethan and Jacobean England,*
1558–1614
Colin Eldridge *The Victorians Overseas*
Richard English *The IRA*
Alan Heesom *The Anglo-Irish Union, 1800–1922*
I. G. C. Hutchison *Scottish Politics in the Twentieth Century*
Gareth Jones *Wales, 1700–1980: Crisis of Identity*
H. S. Jones *Political Thought in Nineteenth-Century Britain*
D. E. Kennedy *The English Revolution, 1642–1649*
Carol Levin *The Reign of Elizabeth I*
Roger Mason *Kingship and Tyranny? Scotland, 1513–1603*
Hiram Morgan *Ireland in the Early Modern Periphery, 1534–1690*
R. C. Nash *English Foreign Trade and the World Economy, 1600–1800*
Robin Prior and Trevor Wilson *Britain and the Impact of World War I*
Brian Quintrell *Government and Politics in Early Stuart England*
Stephen Roberts *Governance in England and Wales, 1603–1688*
David Scott *The British Civil Wars*
John Shaw *The Political History of Eighteenth-Century Scotland*
Alan Sykes *The Radical Right in Britain*
Ann Wiekel *The Elizabethan Counter-Revolution*
Ian Wood *Churchill*

Please note that a sister series, *Social History in Perspective*, is now available.
It covers the key topics in social, cultural and religious history.

British History in Perspective
Series Standing Order
ISBN 0–333–71356–7 hardcover
ISBN 0–333–69331–0 paperback
(*outside North America only*)

You can receive future titles in this series as they are published by placing a standing
order. Please contact your bookseller or, in case of difficulty, write to us at the
address below with your name and address, the title of the series and the ISBN
quoted above.

Customer Services Department, Macmillan Distribution Ltd
Houndmills, Basingstoke, Hampshire RG21 6XS, England

THE TWENTIETH-CENTURY WELFARE STATE

DAVID GLADSTONE

First published in Great Britain 1999 by
MACMILLAN PRESS LTD
Houndmills, Basingstoke, Hampshire RG21 6XS and London
Companies and representatives throughout the world

A catalogue record for this book is available from the British Library.

ISBN 0–333–66920–7 hardcover
ISBN 0–333–66921–5 paperback

 First published in the United States of America 1999 by
ST. MARTIN'S PRESS, INC.,
Scholarly and Reference Division,
175 Fifth Avenue, New York, N.Y. 10010

ISBN 0–312–22087–1

Library of Congress Cataloging-in-Publication Data
Gladstone, David, 1947–
The twentieth-century welfare state / David Gladstone.
p.   cm.
Includes bibliographical references and index.
ISBN 0–312–22087–1 (cloth)
1. Public welfare—Great Britain—History—20th century.   2. Human
services—Great Britain—History—20th century.   3. Welfare state-
-History—20th century.   I. Title.
HV245.G48   1999
361.6'5'09410904—dc21   98–46249
                                                                                CIP

This book is printed on paper suitable for recycling and made from fully managed and
sustained forest sources.

10   9   8   7   6   5   4   3   2   1
08   07   06   05   04   03   02   01   00   99

Printed in Hong Kong

CONTENTS

PREFACE

Welfare states and their future are issues of political concern in many countries. In Britain, for example, the Labour government elected in May 1997 has accorded a high place to welfare reforms in its first year in office. In part, at least, this widespread political reassessment is a recognition of the fact that the context within which welfare policies presently operate is enormously different from the assumptive worlds shared – to greater or lesser degree – by their creators fifty years ago. Then, full employment for men, family stability and national autonomy were defining characteristics of an era in which 'the modern welfare state became an intrinsic part of capitalism's post-war "golden age" ' (Esping-Andersen, 1996, p. 1). Now, that world has been transformed. Globalization, the structure of families, patterns of employment, an ageing population, growing inequalities, as well as the political concern with rising costs, are all part of the changed world of late-twentieth-century welfare. It has been suggested of the British experience that 'these transformations have created new risks which cannot be addressed by Beveridge's "cradle to grave" welfare state, founded on a lifecourse of full-time male employment when interruptions would be predictable and temporary, "dependent" wife and children and a relatively short retirement' (Oppenheim, 1997a, p. 2). It is such an analysis which ostensibly forms the background to the Blair government's comprehensive review of the welfare state and its commitment to an 'active, modern service' and a new welfare contract between citizen and state.

This book, however, is concerned more with Britain's welfare past than its future. Yet there is a strong element of continuity that pervades the twentieth-century discourse on welfare and which underpins some of the current proposals for change: the relationship between work and welfare, the balance of responsibilities between state and citizen, a welfare state based on shared risks and universal entitlements, or one which targets support more selectively to those who need it most. These are not only the continuities inherited from Britain's welfare past. They are also the reality of today's political 'hard choices'.

The growth and changing nature of government activity is a central theme in studies of Britain's twentieth-century welfare experience. The factors that have shaped it, the legislation that has embodied it and some assessment of its performance are, therefore, inevitably part of the narrative of this book. But historical perspectives on Britain's welfare past have increasingly shifted away from a linear progression leading towards the goal of solidaristic, comprehensive state welfare. Rather, they have highlighted the existence of a mixed economy of welfare with a shifting balance between different welfare agencies, in different sectors and at different historical periods. That 'moving frontier' (Finlayson, 1990) provides a perspective on the changing dynamic of the total welfare system. But it also highlights the complex interrelationship of continuity and change within the individual sectors of British welfare in the twentieth century. It is a perspective which structures much of what follows.

I have incurred many debts in writing this book, not least to the wide variety of scholars who have made the study of welfare such a burgeoning and stimulating area of academic inquiry. This book aims to provide a narrative and assessment which draws on the results of such recent research. In the process of blending it into a larger picture, I hope I have maintained at least some of the stimulation of the original. In addition to the research on which it draws, much of what is included here has benefited by presentation to a variety of audiences in this country and elsewhere. Their comment, criticism and discussion has helped to clarify my thinking and to broaden my perspective.

It was Jeremy Black's suggestion that I undertook this study and, though I may have at times regretted the decision as the project grew wider, I am grateful to him and the editorial staff at Macmillan for their patience and forbearance. In its final preparation for the publishers, I am immensely grateful to Carrie Anderson for all her careful, skilful and efficient work. Only my family, however, really know how much has been involved in balancing such a review against a constant stream of other (invariably academic) commitments and demands. It is to them – to Noreen and Alexandra especially – that the book is dedicated.

This book has been completed in the year of the fiftieth anniversary of the postwar creation of the National Health Service and the 'cradle to the grave' system of income maintenance foreshadowed in the 1942

Beveridge Report. Their implementation on 5 July 1948 was hailed in the political 'spin' of the period as 'a day which makes history'. Though the judgement of time may be more ambivalent about what was achieved, that defining moment still exerts its influence on options for the future and the debate about the balance of welfare responsibilities between state and citizen. But it was only part – though an important part – of the longer and more complex story of Britain's twentieth-century welfare past. It is an exploration of that past that we now begin.

University of Bristol   DAVID GLADSTONE

INTRODUCTION

When we study welfare systems we see that they reflect the dominant
cultural and political characteristics in their societies.

(Richard Titmuss, 1987)

At the end of the twentieth century the welfare state remains an undis-
puted feature of British national life. Whether it is defined as a collec-
tion of collectively provided services (Timmins, 1995) or as a synonym
for a particular type of society (Pierson, 1991, p. 7) its activities impinge
upon the lives of the overwhelming majority of the British population
whether as users of its services, tax-paying citizens or employees in the
labour force of the late-twentieth-century welfare state. That is very
different from the position a century ago. Then, despite the growing
intervention of the central and local state that had taken place in the
nineteenth century, many welfare needs were met primarily through
informal networks and formal organisations, most of them outside the
state. These included family and neighbourhood support, philanthropy
and charitable activity, and the organizations of 'respectable' working-
class self-help – the mutual aid and Friendly Societies and trade unions –
which, by the end of the last century, were providing for their members
an embryonic welfare state.

The twentieth century, by contrast, has witnessed a major – though
not uncontentious – expansion of government activity in the supply of
welfare. This welfare state growth has not been confined to Britain. It
has been 'one of the most remarkable social transformations of the
twentieth century world' (Pierson, 1996, p. 100). The result has been a
degree of convergence in welfare systems and a similarity in the range of
risks covered. But 'some welfare states have been significantly more
comprehensive and generous than others' (Baldwin, 1990, p. 6) while
the organizational pattern of welfare state regimes has also differed. Not

1

only are there comparisons to be made between countries. Comparisons over time, for example, suggest a moving frontier (Finlayson, 1990) or a shifting balance between the state and other agencies which comprise the mixed economy of welfare. They also indicate that the role of the state itself is multi-faceted and dynamic.

The popular image is of the state as a direct supplier of services funded from taxation. That model constitutes what Glennerster (1998, p. 329) terms 'old-style welfare statism'. There is general agreement that such direct supply was established partly as the result of legislation passed during the period of the Liberal welfare reforms (1906–14) but principally in the social settlement of the years between 1944 and 1948, the period that 'created' the 'classic welfare state' (Digby, 1989, p. 54). The direct supply of welfare is only one aspect of a more complex system. The state may also pay subsidies to other suppliers. This was a characteristic of the interwar years and has had a continuing role in the welfare state, not least in the last two decades in relation to both the voluntary sector and private providers. More recent developments within the quasi-market include the state funding of non-state organizations such as GP fund-holders to purchase services on behalf of their patients, and the intro-duction of loans to students in higher education. Meanwhile, in addition to its role as a direct supplier of services and as financier of other pro-grammes, the state also acts as a regulator of welfare activities. That role has a history which goes back to the various systems of inspection that were developed during the course of the last century, though it has re-appeared in a modern guise as issues of accountability, quality and choice have become more central to the welfare agenda.

Such an extension and diversification of the state's role such as has occurred this century has significantly re-shaped the structure of Brit-ain's welfare system, not least in terms of the relationship between different welfare producers. In addition, it has drawn more closely together the entity of government and the lives of citizens. 'Until August 1914 a sensible law abiding Englishman could pass through life and hardly notice the existence of the state, beyond the post office and the policeman' (Taylor, 1965, p. 1). Nor for the majority of the population was there any economic relationship between state and citizen. Thresh-olds for the payment of taxes were at levels well above working-class financial capacities and the payment of local taxes (rates on property) were compounded in the rents which most working-class people paid to their landlord. By mid-century that situation had changed considerably, largely as the result of the introduction of more comprehensive welfare services and the inclusion of most manual workers in the income tax system during the Second World War. By then, too, an increasing proportion of the workforce were employed as government or local government officials, many of them in welfare-related occupations such as teachers, workers in the National Health Service or in the delivery of cash benefits.

One further change concerns the politicization of welfare. The emergence of welfare as part of the arena of 'high politics' can be traced to the end of the last century (Harris, 1983a). A century later welfare issues remain central to the political agenda. The Labour government elected in May 1997 has established a wide range of reviews of welfare policy and practice, and has made 'welfare to work' central to its domestic agenda. In addition, Frank Field the Labour MP and former chairman of the Social Security Select Committee, was specifically designated the Minister for Welfare Reform. During his brief period in office before his resignation in July 1998 he observed: 'Attlee's welfare settlement is being transformed and once again this becomes the high politics of our time' (Field, 1997, p. 126). Field's own contribution to this process came in the consultative document (Cm. 3805) *A New Contract for Welfare* published in March 1998. The scenario is of a third way between either dismantling the welfare state or accepting its under-performance. The existing system is depicted as one which 'for many people is increasing their dependence on benefit, rather than helping them to lead independent and fulfilling lives' (p. 1). The third way is based upon 'a new contract between state and citizen' that is designed to provide 'a fair deal, within a system that is clearer, more relevant for the modern world, efficiently run and where costs are manageable' (p. v).

In much the same way as previous Conservative policy, the future shape of Britain's welfare state will depend on the fundamental public spending review which is concurrently in progress and which is scheduled to report later in 1998. But the social security reform especially is located within a moral discourse. In Field's (1997) analysis this centres on the way in which the existing social security provision has an important impact on people's character and behaviour. Means-tested benefits especially, he believes, not only encourage dependency but have a detrimental effect on earning, saving and honesty. Meanwhile, emphasising the welfare-to-work programme, Prime Minister Tony Blair has provided a new vision of the welfare state which offers 'a hand up' to individual independence rather than 'a hand out'.

Work and welfare have been recurrent themes in Britain's welfare past: so too have ideas of contract and citizenship, individual and collective responsibility. Britain's welfare future may rest in the hands of a new cadre of political leaders and the outcome may be further change in the balance of welfare responsibilities between state and citizen. But the parameters of the debate are well-established to anyone familiar with Britain's welfare past

Writing about the Welfare State

There is an extensive literature on the twentieth-century welfare state from a variety of disciplinary perspectives. While it is difficult for any schema fully to capture the diversity of such a literature, the following classification aims to highlight some of the principal features of welfare-state historiography.

The Long March

The long march is characteristic of an early tradition of writing about the welfare state. Reflecting the achievement of the post-Second World War settlement it tended to emphasise the onward march from the Poor Law to the welfare state, from individualism to collectivism, from select-ive services 'reserved for the poor' to a solidaristic, comprehensive and universal welfare state. This style of writing has been characterized (Finlayson, 1994, p. 3) as 'the welfare state escalator', the charting of a progressive path that led onward and upward to the final dénouement of the social legislation of the 1940s.

The limitations of such an approach are now well-established, as is the way in which this model tends to underplay conflict and compromise in the trajectory of the welfare state. But, as Thane (1996, p. 277) has noted,'[t]o describe the undeniable growth of state action in the field of welfare through the century is not necessarily to claim that it was direc-ted towards improvement, it is merely to point out that it happened'.

Crowding Out

Much of the historical writing about welfare in the post-1945 period tended disproportionately to concentrate on state activity. To that extent it 'crowded out' the continuities and changing environment of other facets of welfare supply: the role of families and informal support, the private market and the diversity represented by the voluntary sector.

It was only in the 1980s when the welfare state came under sustained political attack that historians seriously began to rediscover those arenas of welfare experience that they had hitherto neglected or ignored. As Daunton (1996a, p. 1) points out, not only have the political developments of the 1980s and 1990s laid to rest the teleological interpretations of the welfare state, in addition in historical writing they have 'produced a much greater sensitivity to the wide range of possibilities in coping with risks in society'. A recent study (Johnson, 1996, p. 227) suggests that social risks relate to health, the life-cycle, economy and environment, and argues that 'the strategies adopted to accommodate these risks, whether individual or collective, private or public, form the welfare structures of any society'. The emphasis is thus increasingly on the mixed economy of welfare in the past as well as the present, and 'the moving frontier' (Finalyson, 1990) between sectors of welfare supply.

And the Rest of the World

In much of the earlier historical writing it was by no means uncommon to find Britain hailed as the first and most comprehensive welfare state. That view has been challenged as the result of more recent comparative historical studies. Most of the advanced Western European nations, for example, had constructed some form of welfare state in the years between the wars, while after 1945 'social policy had become an integral part of the institutional life of each democracy' (Ashford, 1986, p. 297). Such comparative studies highlighted national differences as well as certain common features of the welfare-state experience, such as its place in industrialization and modernization, political enfranchisement and levels of economic prosperity. Comparison highlights similarities and differences in the present as well as in the past. Esping-Andersen (1996, Ch. 1) has recently noted the similar challenges facing modern welfare states. These include 'the growing dysfunction between existing social protection schemes and evolving needs and risks' consequent on changes in family structure, employment patterns and the life-cycle. Along with globalization, de-industrialization and an ageing population these are common experiences in many welfare states. Yet the pattern of response to such changes, he suggests, has varied in different welfare-state regimes. Esping-Andersen himself contrasts Scandinavia with the

Anglo-Saxon countries including Britain and the USA and the countries of continental Europe.

Much of this research, however, is based on a small number of Western industrialized or capitalist societies. Walker and Wong (1996, p. 67) have recently criticised this perspective, suggesting that it is 'ethnocentric western social research' that has determined 'the social construction of welfare and the welfare state in both academic and popular discourses'.

And Women Too

> We have come to learn how social policies...are often shaped by...normative assumptions about gender roles, in particular about the sexual division of labour and of social responsibility, with its primary assumption of female dependency on male earning power. Also about how, reciprocally...social welfare policies shape, reinforce and perpetuate such roles. (Thane, 1991a, p. 93)

That position represents a considerable shift from earlier postwar analyses of social policies when, compared to social class, both family and gender were neglected. Those working within a gender perspective have both reassessed the role of women's agency in the creation of welfare states and highlighted the ambiguities and disadvantages of women's place within the contemporary welfare system. These dimensions are by now well-known: the ideology of womanhood on which the Beveridge Report and much of the social security legislation of the 1940s was based; and the disadvantages which women experience both as consumers of welfare and as carers.

More recent studies have also examined women's agency in the production of welfare. That too has resulted from a greater focus upon the mixed economy of welfare which has emphasised the importance of the domestic domain in welfare production. But during the twentieth century women have also been increasingly engaged in the formal sector of welfare employment. The increase in the number of welfare-related occupations that has taken place over that time has both enhanced women's financial independence and extended their opportunities for paid employment outside the home. An alternative view suggests, however, that women's welfare work has tended to replicate in the paid labour market a gendered set of domestic skills, and contrasts the occupational segregation that often exists between women and men in the formal sector of welfare employment. For all these reasons it has become impossible 'to evaluate the welfare state without understanding how it deals with women' (Digby and Stewart, 1996, p. 23).

Plan of the Book

The first four chapters of this book examine chronologically Britain's welfare state during the course of the twentieth century. Chapter 1 discusses the emergent collectivism in the period up to the outbreak of the Second World War in 1939, while wartime experiences, the Beveridge Report and the new arrangements for welfare introduced in the 1940s are the subject of Chapter 2. Retrospectively, there has been much discussion of the so-called consensus that for a period of 30 years from the mid-1940s apparently united the wartime Coalition Government and its successor Labour and Conservative peacetime administrations. More recent research, however, suggests that 'the idea of consensus obscures much more than it illuminates' (Jones and Kandiah, 1996, p. x). This debate will be examined in Chapter 3 which focuses on the adaptations and changing fortunes of the welfare state as wartime austerity gave way to increased affluence for a significant proportion of the population. Whether the notion of consensus is accepted or not, there is considerable agreement that from the mid-1970s the welfare state entered a period of reappraisal. On the one hand there was a crisis of political legitimacy and popular support. On the other a change in the discourse of welfare and in its organizational structures which called into question the solidaristic and comprehensive vision of the 1940s. This changing welfare paradigm forms the subject of Chapter 4.

The remaining chapters examine the financing of welfare, its expanding and changing labour force and the distributional impact of the welfare state in terms of gender, class and generation. The economics of the welfare state has been one of the continuities of political concern over the past century. Changes over that time both in the pattern of raising revenue and spending it will be the subject of Chapter 5. Over the same period, the welfare state has significantly contributed to Britain's changing employment profile. It has made a significant contribution to the expansion of white collar and white blouse occupations. More recently the notion on which the classic welfare state was founded – that the professional worker and administrative bureaucrat knows best – has increasingly been called into question by a more assertive consumerism and the political rhetoric of individual choice. That aspect forms part of the discussion in Chapter 6. Chapter 7 draws on several decades of increasingly sophisticated evaluation studies to present an assessment of Britain's welfare state. How far has it mitigated – or reinforced – the socially structured stratifications of gender, age and class? At the century's end, what are the risks, and the incidence of those risks, that threaten the condition of individual and collective well-being: and what are the contours of disadvantage?

1

ANTECEDENTS

> Now government is the organised expression of the wishes and wants
> of the people and under those circumstances let us cease to regard it
> with suspicion... Now it is our business to extend its functions and to
> see in what ways its operations can be usefully enlarged.
>
> (Joseph Chamberlain, 1914)

The quest for origins is a never-ending task. That applies to the welfare
state as much as to other aspects of historical experience. De Schweinitz
traced England's road to social security back to the Statute of Labourers
of 1348. Many other studies of Britain's welfare inheritance have
focused on the growing codification of the Poor Law that occurred
during the sixteenth century. Yet another tradition of historical writing
locates the growing encroachment of the state's welfare activity in the
nineteenth century, linking it to the concurrent historical processes of
industrialization, urbanization and the extension of political democracy.
The twentieth-century welfare state – as well as the debate about welfare
– has been shaped by each of these antecedents. But central to that
century's experience has been the extension and changing role of the
public sector in welfare supply.

Welfare and the Public Sector

'In 1900 only paupers were in immediate receipt of public munificence,
and only school children in regular contact with public sector

employees – their teachers' (Johnson, 1994b, p. 479). By the outbreak of the Second World War the situation was very different. 'Never before', a report on the British Social Services pointed out in 1937, 'have the public services of the state been so continuously and intimately bound up with the family life of ordinary citizens as they have in recent years' (PEP, 1937, p. 10). This was reflected both by increased expenditure and an expansion in the range of services available. The PEP *Report* estimated that total expenditure on public welfare services had increased from £35.3 million in 1900 to £400.8 million in 1934. Per head of population that represented an increase from 19s 2d in 1900 to £8 16s in 1934. In addition, over the same period the range of services had considerably expanded. The *Report* divided them into three categories. First were what it termed 'constructive community services' such as education, public health and medical services, and the employment exchanges and training centres of the Ministry of Labour. Secondly, the social insurance scheme introduced in 1911, the widows', orphans' and old age contributory pensions introduced in 1925 and the scheme of workman's compensation. Finally there were the social assistance services which included the non-contributory old age pensions introduced in 1908, the allowances of the Unemployment Assistance Board and the services of the local Public Assistance authorities which had superceded the poor law in 1929.

The result of this expansion in public welfare was a paradox. On the one hand 'the working class which entered the Second World War could call upon the resources of the state for material support more comprehensively than their predecessors in 1914' (Crowther, 1988, p. 73). On the other, the web of welfare was of considerable complexity. It encompassed cash benefits and direct services, supplied both by central and local government and financed through direct as well as indirect taxation. If the range of welfare services had expanded such that 'they vitally affect the great majority of British citizens', their incremental and unplanned expansion had made them by the late 1930s, 'so unwieldy at present that they are virtually uncontrollable' (PEP, 1937, p. 180). It is interesting to remember that the Beveridge Report (1942), which became the most potent symbol of Britain's welfare future, began as an inquiry into 'the wide range of anomalies that had arisen as a result of the haphazard and piecemeal growth of the social security system over the previous fifty years' (Harris, 1977, p. 378).

The welfare state of the 1940s, however, went beyond administrative rationalization. It created a system of public welfare 'more centralized and much more comprehensive in terms of the proportion of the population and the type of social contingencies covered' (Johnson, 1994a, p. 285). But in the process it extended the public responsibility for needs and socially constructed dependencies that had antecedents earlier in the century. It is this recognition of public responsibility – for children, for adults (especially men) of working age and for older people – that will be discussed in the next sections.

Welfare, the Public Sector and Children

Four Acts of Parliament passed between 1902 and 1908 defined the changing relationship between the public sector and children. In the process they extended the legislative concerns of the later nineteenth century and mapped out a new terrain which perceived children as investments (Hendrick, 1994, 1997). The 1902 Education Act rationalized the system of schooling, though it provoked considerable Liberal and nonconformist hostility. Much local diversity was replaced by a more streamlined administration under the control of local education authorities. Those authorities were also made responsible for post-elementary education in the public sector, thereby initiating a pattern of schools and access to them which was to continue until the 1944 Education Act. In practice, this divided public education into two types: an elementary system which was grant-aided from public funds, and a secondary sector which charged fees. This division has been portrayed (Simon, 1965, p. 239) as imposing 'within the state supported system of English education an hierarchic structure of schooling corresponding to social class divisions'. From 1907, however, in order to qualify for a state grant secondary schools had to admit without charge up to a quarter of their children from the elementary sector who had successfully passed an attainment test at the age of 11. This gradually increased the proportion of working-class children in the secondary sector, but the prevailing impression remained of an educational system divided along the lines of social class.

The legislation of the early twentieth century concerned children's bodies as well as their minds. By the 1906 Education (Provision of Meals) Act local authorities were empowered to provide facilities for school meals for necessitous school children and were allowed to levy a halfpenny rate for the purpose. In 1914 this provision became compulsory. The introduction of school meals generated considerable controversy since there was to be no penalty of disenfranchisement, such as happened to those receiving poor relief. The General Secretary of the Charity Organisation Society, C. S. Loch, 'stressed the temptation school meals posed to mothers to neglect their children's welfare'. But there were others, also affiliated to the COS such as Helen Bosanquet and other women social investigators, who felt that 'the real danger was the more fragile male incentive to provide' (Lewis, 1995, p. 63).

The Act introducing school medical inspection in 1907 similarly laid an added duty on the local education authorities and the following year a circular invited them to establish school clinics. Harris (1995a) has suggested that the school medical service was hampered before the First World War by the absence of any earmarked funds until 1912, and has shown how even in the interwar years there was considerable variation in the service available. But by then child health and welfare 'was serving as a powerful argument for extending the role of the state in health and welfare generally' (Cooter, 1992, p. 32).

The final measure relating specifically to children was the 1908 Children Act, known as the Children's Charter. This consolidated the legislation of the previous half century concerning the treatment of children both by the law and their parents. In addition to the creation of a separate system of juvenile justice, considerable regulatory and supervisory duties were placed upon local authorities. As such it was part of the process which brought about 'a major restructuring of the legal relations between husbands and wives, parents and children, the family and the state' (Harris, 1993, p. 75).

Welfare, the Public Sector and Adults of Working Age

The legislation for children was primarily preventive, whereas measures for adults redefined the relationship between work and welfare. In this context there were two alternative inheritances from the nineteenth century. On the one hand was the belief that 'the economy was ... perfectly capable of absorbing all those who sought work' (Scott, 1994, p. 7). This view, symbolized by the New Poor Law of 1834, regarded unemployment as a personal unwillingness to work. On the other, was the later nineteenth-century recognition of 'categories of people in need (that is the normally industrious) for whom the deterrent and degrading Poor Law was inappropriate' (Harris, 1972, p. 147). Embodied in measures such as Chamberlain's 1886 public works circular, this view of unemployment regarded it more as a structural question than an issue of personal failing, the consequence of trade cycles and economic conditions over which individuals had little if any control.

It was William Beveridge who provided one of the most sophisticated analyses of this new approach in his book significantly entitled *Unemployment: A Problem of Industry* (1909). And it was Beveridge the civil servant, working with Winston Churchill as President of the Board of Trade, who introduced labour exchanges in 1909 as a means of reducing the problem of frictional unemployment:

> If properly worked, he believed, these could become the instrument by which casual labour, with its casual and irregular way of life, would be replaced by regularly employed workers able to lead a life of respectability and to swell the ranks of organised labour. (Hennock, 1994, p. 88)

Labour exchanges, state-run by the Board of Trade and nationally financed, were a significant shift away from the attitudes of 1834. But as Clarke (1996, p. 59) notes, their introduction 'was hardly socialism: it was a means of making the free market in labour work more efficiently by means of a little interventionist lubrication'.

Labour exchanges became central to the operation of unemployment benefits under the 1911 National Insurance Act since they 'established a test of willingness to work and [were] thus a passport to benefits' (*ibid.*, p. 60). The contractual scheme conceived in 1911 was limited to the 2.5 million workers in seven trades such as shipbuilding, engineering and the construction industry where workers were particularly exposed to the interruption of earnings caused by temporary cyclical unemployment. Progressively, however, during the interwar years coverage was extended to almost all manual workers, though since benefits were restricted to 26 weeks in any one year it was largely irrelevant to the long-term unemployment of the time. Another of the scheme's limitations concerned the level of benefit that was paid. It was both lower than some existing trade union schemes and less than the amount of outdoor relief. Its purpose was 'only to tide the workman over short periods of unemployment, not to support him for any length of time' (Crowther, 1988, p. 33). It is hardly surprising, therefore, that during the interwar years 'a scheme originally restricted mainly to skilled workers and initiated during a period of high employment was found wanting' (Johnson, 1996, p. 242).

The other part of the 1911 National Insurance Act dealt with health insurance reflecting the view that 'ill health threw too many respectable people on to the Poor Law and caused the loss of many working days' (Thane, 1996, p. 78). Politically it proved much more contentious than unemployment insurance, principally because of the range of vested interests such as Friendly Societies and medical aid organisations who were already providing their members with medical attention and sick pay. Benefits offered varied between the different organisations, and the very poor tended to be excluded because of the contribution requirements. Lloyd George's health insurance scheme aimed to be more comprehensive. In return for contributions from employers, workers and the Treasury through taxation, it offered sickness benefits and basic GP care to those earning less than a specified minimum annual income – but not to their families and dependants. Meanwhile, as a concession to those who had hitherto operated health insurance programmes the scheme was administered by centrally-registered approved societies (Friendly Societies, commercial insurance companies and some trade unions). These societies managed sickness pay benefits and paid the doctor selected from a panel organised by Local Insurance Commissions. The numbers covered by the scheme considerably increased, from 11.5 million in 1912 to 20.2 million in 1938 by which time 42 per cent of the population was included in the health insurance scheme. This expansion owed much to population growth, the raising of the ceiling on minimum annual earnings and the increased coverage of women (Whiteside, 1998).

With financial payments of 7s (35p) per week for unemployment benefit and 10s (50p) for health insurance, the state insurance scheme represented a significant innovation in Britain's response to the economic risks occasioned by unemployment and ill-health. But the scheme was not without its critics who condemned its compulsion and loss of democratic control. The contributory basis of the insurance scheme meanwhile meant that 'the state was to be the partner of the poor, not their sole provider' (Vincent, 1991, p. 41). As Harris (1993, p. 218) notes, 'ministers influenced by "new liberal" ideas about redistribution and collective provision were equally concerned with buttressing "old liberal" ideas about independence and personal saving'.

Welfare, the Public Sector and Old Age

The Old Age Pensions Act 1908 marked the culmination of thirty years public and political discussion about financial provision for older people (Thane, 1978). As life expectancy increased, so too did the visibility of the poverty that invariably accompanied old age. For Rowntree (1902, p. 136) it was a time when the labourer sank 'back again into poverty when his children have married and left him and he himself is too old to work, for his income has never permitted his saving enough for him and his wife to live upon for more than a short time'.

In the absence of any pension provision the alternative means of financial support were the Poor Law, on which a considerable proportion of older people relied in their final years, private charity and in some cases extended sickness benefit from Friendly Societies which served as an incipient old-age pension. The Friendly Societies in particular initially opposed the introduction of state old-age pensions as a threat to their welfare nexus. But as their financial difficulties worsened towards the end of the 1890s, their opposition became more muted. There was, however, a broader ideological questioning of old-age pensions which formed an important ingredient to the political discussion. 'Could the state intervene to help the most deprived without undercutting self-help; in particular, would non-contributory pensions parch the springs of thrift and harm work-incentives by undercutting the less-eligibility principle of the Poor Law?' (Digby, 1989, p. 46).

When it was introduced in 1908 the Old Age Pensions Act was based both on a test of means and of character eligibility. Despite this, almost 100 000 more qualified for the old-age pension in its first year than the original estimate of 572 000; and in 1911 the exclusion of those receiving poor relief was abandoned which added 122 000 aged paupers to the scheme. These two factors created extra costs which, since the scheme was non-contributory, had to be met by the Treasury. It has been suggested that it was these extra costs which made insurance a more attractive proposition to fund sickness and unemployment schemes since contributions from employers and employees limited Treasury liability. Pensions themselves became part of the contributory national insurance scheme in 1925, when widows' and orphans' pensions were also introduced.

Old age pensions 'marked an important step in the development of central state welfare services' (Johnson, 1996, p. 238). But when they were introduced, their level was far from generous. Five shillings (25p), the amount of the full pension, represented about one-fifth of the average labourer's wage and 'would just about feed and clothe a parsimonious couple... What was given made it easier for the poor to arrange their income over time, what was withheld forced them to do so' (Vincent, 1991, p. 41).

Explaining the Expansion

A range of explanations has been advanced to account for the expansion in the public sector of welfare in the early twentieth century. This section can do no more than to highlight some of the principal contributions.

It is important to note first of all that the pre-First World War welfare legislation built upon a pattern of government intervention that had already been established during the previous century. A whole corpus of historical studies has portrayed 'the nineteenth century revolution in government' (for example MacDonagh, 1958, 1977; Roberts, 1960) which, 'acquiring its own momentum carried state intervention forward despite ideological and political resistance through the middle years of the nineteenth century' (Thane, 1990, p. 19). From the 1880s, however, the welfare activities of government became both more proactive and high profile. Thane (1996, p. 42) refers to the number and range of Royal Commissions and Select Committees that were appointed in the 1880s and 1890s to investigate aspects of what the earlier Victorians would have termed 'the condition of the people question'. Similarly Harris (1983a) has shown how welfare became a matter of 'high politics' in the years between 1880 and 1914. Social policy issues featured more on Cabinet agenda and social policy departments became increasingly attractive to talented up-coming politicians. Among the best known were David Lloyd George and Winston Churchill, two of the prime movers in the Liberal welfare reform programme between 1906 and 1911.

Simultaneously, as a result of the early-twentieth-century debate on national efficiency, social policy came to be seen as complementary to other areas of government and public concern, particularly the role and defence of the Empire and international economic competitiveness. Evidence about the physical condition of recruits for the Boer War (1899–1902) highlighted the interrelationship between welfare and Empire:

While the news from South Africa of military failures reflected the incompetence, amateurishness and deficient education of the officers, the news at home of eager but unfit recruits reflected the physical debility and ill health of would-be soldiers. If the graph of a dropping birth rate was perceived as an omen of an expected (future) imperial decline, the recruitment statistics were a statement of immediate national poverty. (Dwork, 1987, p. 11)

As a result of the evidence from the recruitment centres, 'Edwardians increasingly recognised the need for a healthy and expanding popula- tion to populate and defend the Empire' (Harrison, 1996, p. 67). In this way it becomes possible to explain the legislation that followed the Inter-Departmental Committee on Physical Deterioration (1904) con- cerned with preventive services for the health and nutrition of school children.

Increasingly, commercial competitiveness from other countries also contained a welfare message. ' "The stress and keenness of international competition"... was to raise poverty – a poverty that could result in a nation unfit to retain its share of the world market – into a matter of urgent national interest' (Hennock, 1994, p. 80). That 'urgent national interest' was informed by evidence from the poverty studies conducted in London by Charles Booth and by Seebohm Rowntree's study of York carried out in the late 1890s. These studies were part of the contribution of empirical social investigation to the contemporary concern with 'pov- erty in the midst of plenty'; and represented an attempt to answer the question famously posed in the Fabian Society pamphlet of 1884 *Why are the Many Poor?* Rowntree's investigation laid the foundation for much subsequent sociological research with its construction of the poverty line, the distinction between primary and secondary poverty and the notion of the life-cycle of poverty. But:

his discovery that every labourer with a normal sized family of three children passed through a period of ten years when he and his family would be underfed had implications both for the fitness of the next generation and for the efficiency of the present labour force. (Hen- nock, 1994, p. 80)

As a strategy of political action 'the quest for national efficiency' had a wide-ranging appeal. Not only did it offer the potential of fitter and healthier soldiers and workers, it offered to the working class 'more rapid progress towards social improvement and a fairer society than they could have achieved by their own unaided efforts'. Perkin (1989, pp. 159–60), however, believes that for the burgeoning professional classes there was 'perhaps the greatest prize of all, a share in the expansion of expert services provided by or paid for by government [and] a higher level of remuneration guaranteed by the state'. Public welfare thus 'enlisted middle class self-interest as well as altruism' (Harrison, 1996, p. 71).

If the context was becoming more conducive to greater collectivism, the welfare reforms introduced by the Liberal government (1906–14) have also been explained in terms of political pragmatism and the ideological change of New Liberalism. The Liberals received an overwhelming majority in the general election of 1906. But their manifesto contained no commitment to any specific measure of social reform (Craig, 1975, pp. 10–13). The first phase of their programme (1906–8) owed much to the consensus created by the Report of the Inter-Departmental Committee on Physical Deterioration (1904) and to back bench pressure. It was only with the introduction of labour exchanges and, more especially, with the beginnings of the insurance scheme in 1911 that the Liberals began to march forward into the 'untrodden fields' of social policy. This transition has been explained by a number of political factors: the presence in the 1906 Parliament of 53 Labour MPs who represented a challenge to the traditional working-class support for the Liberal Party; the by-election reverses in which Liberal seats were lost to Labour; the reconstruction of the Cabinet in 1908 which brought Lloyd George and Winston Churchill to the positions respectively of Chancellor of the Exchequer and President of the Board of Trade; their shared view that social reform was both desirable – to provide a more extensive provision against the risks of an industrial society – and necessary – as an antidote to socialism. On both these counts the 1911 National Insurance Act is especially significant. 'Insurance was the capitalist's answer to the problem of want, and by reducing it insurance covered up what the socialist saw as the root cause of poverty' (Fraser, 1984, pp. 163–4).

Enlarging the role of the state in welfare, however, represented a significant move away from the individualism and *laissez-faire* of nineteenth-century liberalism. The bridge between the two is usually attributed to the ideology of New Liberalism and in particular to the Oxford philosopher T.H. Green. Though Green himself remained committed to voluntary effort, he 'contributed to the climate of political argument in Britain . . . a distinctive tone of earnestness, social concern and addiction to principle' (Barker, 1997, p. 23). As he identified it in the 1880s, the new arena of freedom with which liberals had to concern themselves was the freedom of each person to develop their capabilities and to realize themselves in self-fulfilment. And in that process, Green contended, the state had a positive role to play by removing the obstacles that threatened an individual's freedom:

> Our modern legislation, then, with reference to labour and education and health involving as it does manifold interference with freedom of contract is justified on the ground that it is the business of the state to maintain the conditions without which a free exercise of human faculties is impossible. (cited in Greenleaf, 1983, p. 136)

The nature of Green's influence on the world of practical politics has been questioned (Freeden, 1990, pp. 18–20); but Perkin (1989, p. 127) has suggested that his ideas of positive rather than negative freedom appealed especially to those middle-class men and women who found his 'politics of conscience' and the service of humanity an ethical substitute for their declining religious faith.

Reactions to the Expanding State

So far this chapter has outlined some of the principal welfare legislation of the early twentieth century and some of the explanations that have been advanced to account for the growing collectivism of the period. This section examines some of the reactions to this reconfiguration of the relationship between the state and its citizens.

Social reform was supported by Conservative, Liberal and Labour politicians, though there were significant differences of opinion between them as recent studies have shown. Green (1996, pp. 228–34) has indicated the variety of theoretical positions on the role of the state within the early-twentieth-century Conservative Party, though by the Edwardian period the dominant strand was that of collectivism. That, however, did not prevent 'Conservatives of all hues' fearing that the Liberal welfare programme represented 'a way to mobilise popular opinion on the basis of electoral bribery funded by a "confiscatory" tax regime' (ibid., p. 236). In Chamberlain's tariff reform programme the Conservatives had an alternative route to social reform. As a result 'protectionism proved to be instrumental in drawing the Tory Party towards the twentieth century notion of the state with its responsibility for managing the economy and maintaining the living standards of the people' (Pugh, 1988, p. 279).

Labour's inheritance on the issue of social reform was diverse (Thane, 1984). It polarized between accepting the benefit of material improvement among the working class on the one hand and, on the other, seeing state social reform as 'part of the capitalist strategy to defeat socialism and keep the working classes in subjection' (ibid., p. 882). The Liberal welfare reforms intensified these previous divisions, but after 1906 'the stance most characteristic of organised labour... was one of support for the Liberal reforms, whilst stressing their inadequacy and pressing both for improvement and for maximum working class participation in their administration' (ibid., p. 897).

As we have already noted, the Liberal's programme was far removed from the values of traditional liberal individualism and there were those such as Hillaire Belloc, G. K. Chesterton and A.V. Dicey who opposed the tendency of the centralizing state. In *The Servile State* (1912) Belloc was critical of a society in which 'the mass of men are "constrained by law to labour to the profit of a minority" while receiving as compensation "a security which the Old Capitalism did not give them"' (Greenleaf, 1983, p. 92). Both conditions threatened freedom, and in their place Belloc advocated a distributive state in which political and social freedom would be secured by a wide dispersion of property.

What then of working-class and business attitudes to welfare and its reform?

Much of the literature has highlighted how the state was synonymous with control to many in the working class. Factory and Education Acts had threatened the precarious budgets of Victorian working-class families; health visitors and sanitary inspectors made 'uninvited intrusions on the privacy of the home' while their high-minded advice 'was absurdly irrelevant to the poverty of its recipients' (Thompson, 1988, p. 357). State responsibility for welfare, moreover, threatened the institutions of working-class self-help and mutual aid and the values on which they were established, which rigorously distinguished the 'respectable' from the 'rough' working class (Harris, 1992a, p. 177). Support for measures of welfare reform was varied. The introduction of old-age pensions was a more popular measure than either the reforms affecting children or the initial response to the 1911 National

Insurance legislation. But in general, 'regular work and wages sufficient for a decent life' to permit saving and to maintain independence summarizes the feelings of working-class people (Thane, 1984, p. 899).

The ambivalence and diversity that characterized working-class attitudes was also apparent among the representatives of employers:

> At one end of the spectrum was the repression of socialist movements and militant trade unionism, at the other was the promotion of a moral and ideological consensus as to the inseparable links between capital and labour, and hence of capitalism as a social system. (Hay, 1977, p. 436)

Those espousing the latter view increasingly concerned themselves in Chambers of Commerce with issues such as unemployment, technical education, old-age pensions and the future of the Poor Law. Their expectation of state welfare was that it would contribute to industrial efficiency and discriminate between the 'rough' and 'respectable' sections of the working class. Its apparent failure to do so, together with the rising costs of welfare compared to competitor countries, meant that 'the weight of organised employer opinion was increasingly thrown against state welfare in the inter-war period' (Hay, 1978, p. 121).

The First World War and its Impact

There is an extensive literature on the relationship between war and welfare. We have already noted the effect of the Boer War in highlighting the debate about Britain's imperial and commercial decline; while the experiences of the Second World War helped to shape the solidaristic nature of the postwar welfare state. The impact of the First World War (1914–18) lay in the transformation of the British state and in making the expansion of government more acceptable. In that respect 'the Second World War merely reaped what the First World War had sown' (Lowe, 1995, p. 33).

During the war new government ministries were created, new boards and commissions established and the Cabinet secretariat was established to coordinate the growing range of government activities. At least until after the war, the Treasury lost its supremacy over Whitehall departments and its detailed control over public expenditure. Extra civil servants were employed and businessmen were recruited into Whitehall and the government. This more dynamic government impinged directly upon the population – not least through food rationing, rent control and the regulation and direction of labour. Meanwhile, as a result of wartime inflation and rising wage rates, considerable numbers of working men became liable to income tax for the first time.

There was no guarantee that such an expanded government would continue after the war was over. It lacked intellectual foundation. As Tawney noted, 'war collectivism had not been accompanied by any intellectual conversion on the subject of the proper relations between the state and economic life, while it did not last long enough to change social habits' (cited De Groot, 1996, p. 327). More practically, the legislation which had established the big interventionist ministries, such as Food and Munitions, was time limited. 'Rolling back the state was therefore a passive act which consisted of letting deadlines run' (*ibid*., p. 327). In addition, there was a powerful view of reconstruction which perceived it as a return to 'pre-war normality' and which questioned whether, with its extensive postwar debt, Britain had the capacity to afford more collectivist measures of social improvement.

Despite these countervailing forces, the momentum of social reform continued. Wartime exigencies led the government to pay allowances to the wives and children of soldiers and pensions to civilian dependants of those who had been injured, while 'the huge loss of young men during the war made governments even more concerned to promote the health of infants and to make motherhood less burdensome' (Pugh, 1994, p. 155). The result was an expansion in the number of maternity and child welfare clinics as well as of health visitors, while the 1918 Maternity and Child Welfare Act finally ended the inter-departmental rivalry between the Local Government Board and the Board of Education (Harris, 1995a, pp. 77–9). Immediately after the war, Fisher's Education Act 'encouraged the Board of Education and the local authorities to build up an all-embracing system of education from nursery schools to adult evening classes' while increasing the school leaving age to 14 (Stevenson, 1984, p. 248). In the following year, the 1919 Housing and Town Planning Act gave a generous state subsidy to local authorities to encourage house building. In the same year a separate Ministry of Health was established (Honingsbaum, 1989) and in 1920 the Unemployment Insurance Act considerably extended the limited prewar scheme introduced in 1911. Politically, however, the postwar depression that began in 1920 weakened 'the advocates for reconstruction in the Coalition

Government and exposed them to more conservative forces' (Crowther, 1988, p. 38). Both education and the 'homes fit for heroes' programme became victims of the 'Geddes axe' and the postwar reassertion of Treasury control with its commitment to balanced budgets and high interest rates in preparation for Britain's return to the gold standard (Burk, 1982; Middleton, 1996a).

The Interwar Years

The 1920s and 1930s are characterized by a paradox. The popular perception is of economic decline and recession and large-scale unemployment. That view, however, has to be balanced by rising wage levels for most of the period for those who were in work, new employment opportunities in car production, light engineering and service industries, the spread of home ownership and the increasing acquisition of consumer goods.

In a political sense, however, 'unemployment is the problem which dominates inter-war social policy' (Crowther, 1988, p. 40). Between 1921 and 1938 the official unemployment total never fell below one million and it is generally agreed that the unofficial total was significantly higher. The unemployment of the period was both cyclical – as in 1921 when the postwar boom burst and in 1931–3 when the British economy experienced the impact of the Wall Street crash of 1929 – and structural, resulting from the loss of markets and increased international competition. As a result, the experience of unemployment was especially severe in those areas of the country which, in the nineteenth century, had been 'the workshop of the world'. The unemployment figures thus highlight the contrast between the increasingly prosperous and growing communities of the south of England and the Midlands, and the industrial graveyards of South Wales, Central Scotland and the north and west of England.

It was a contrast widely revealed in the social surveys of the period, for example *Men without Work* (Pilgrim Trust, 1938). To them has been attributed 'a diffused acceptance of the legitimacy of a more "forward" role for the state' (Supple, 1993, pp. 380–1) and an important role in the campaign for social reconstruction which developed further during the Second World War (B. Harris, 1994, p. 213). But as the record of the interwar years shows, unemployment also generated much government activity. This involved both the unemployment insurance scheme and the Poor Law/assistance tradition, both of which were considerably remodelled during the interwar period.

After its extension in 1920 and 1921, approximately 11 million workers and their families were covered by the insurance scheme. Such an expansion generated additional financial pressure and the 'genuinely seeking work test' was introduced to ensure that benefits were restricted to the deserving unemployed. The tightening of the test after 1925 and the numbers of those who were refused benefit has led one assessment (Deacon, 1987, p. 35) to conclude that 'the test was . . . an effective, if not savage, method of ensuring that work incentives were maintained in a period of mass unemployment, and that the cost of benefits was kept to a minimum'. Despite these safeguards however, in the late 1920s and early 1930s the insurance fund moved further into deficit, from £25 million in 1928 to £125 million in 1931. In line with the May Committee's recommendation for a reduction in benefit payments, which the Labour Government was unwilling to implement, the subsequent National Government imposed a 10 per cent cut (restored in 1934) in 1931. At the same time contributions were raised and the benefit period reduced. There were, however, other changes which moved the system further away from the principles of commercial insurance. These were the payment of additional benefits to those who had exhausted their entitlement to unemployment insurance benefit. These additions were variously labelled uncovenanted (1921), extended (1924) and transitional (1927) benefits and, after 1931, transitional payments. By these benefits 'the government nurtured the belief that the insurance scheme was concerned less with "tiding over" individuals temporarily out of work than with providing adequate living standards for the unemployed' (Garside, 1990, p. 41). But despite all this manoeuvring 'the government was still without any systematic policy towards relief of the able bodied unemployed' (*ibid.*, p. 51).

Financial assistance was also available through the Poor Law to three principal groups: those who had exhausted their entitlement to any insurance benefit; those who needed to have their benefit payments 'topped up' as, for example, when a family member was ill; and those who had not been in employment long enough to claim insurance benefit. At the end of the 1920s the Poor Law was *de facto* abolished and its responsibilities transferred to the Public Assistance Committees of the larger local authorities. As such, it marked 'the climax of Chamberlain's strategy to enlarge and rationalize local government'

(Crowther, 1988, p. 49), but in the process it transferred the administration of relief from locally elected Guardians to larger units of local government. In that milieu, it has been suggested 'the voices of those who received so much from the rates would be drowned out by the cries of those who contributed so much' (Vincent, 1991, p. 61).

The tension between the centre and the localities which had been a long-standing feature of the Poor Law was finally brought to an end by the Unemployment Act of 1934. The distinction between insurance and assistance benefits which it introduced presaged the structure of the income maintenance system introduced by the post-Second World War Labour government. But as local authority financial assistance faded away, it also meant that 'thereafter the major part of the cost of unemployment relief would be shouldered by central government' (Garside, 1990, p. 81) with the Unemployment Assistance Board acting as 'a buffer between the government and those demanding more generous benefits' (*ibid.*, pp. 73–4).

Central control was also increased in the operation of the health insurance scheme. Whiteside (1998) has argued that during the interwar period the autonomy of the Approved Societies was progressively eroded. 'Constant changes in the regulations governing the rights of the unemployed with varying contributory status, of women claimants, of voluntary contributors or members aged over 65 – all increased the authority of those few Whitehall officials who governed the scheme'. Their control was further reinforced by the interwar recession which 'reduced contributory income, raised the incidence of claims [and] generated cuts in public spending'. The Approved Societies thus became 'private agencies for public purposes', and between them the Government Actuary and the Treasury effectively stopped any extension of health insurance during the interwar period (Whiteside, 1983, pp. 165–93). It is generally acknowledged that there were many limitations in the health insurance scheme; these included restrictions on treatment and the exclusion of dependants (Webster, 1988a, p. 11). But whereas other writers have attributed the eventual demise of the Approved Societies in the 1940s to the administrative complexity of the system itself, Whiteside (1998) believes that 'tight central regulation and the vulnerability of the scheme's finances to public expenditure controls' also needs to be taken into account.

While central government was increasing its administrative control over financial welfare in the conditions of interwar recession, it appeared content to leave other aspects of the expanding welfare programme to local authorities. Yet they too 'took on their expanded functions in the context of mounting central control' (Harrison, 1996, p. 119) and the increasing subvention of local authority activity by central government finance. Between the outbreak of the First and Second World Wars central government grants rose from 22 per cent of total local authority expenditure to 41 per cent (Stevenson, 1984, p. 308). The post-First World War housing programme, designed to provide 'homes for heroes' for example, 'introduced the first large scale government subsidy to local house building' (Thane, 1996, p. 136) while the slum-clearance programme launched in 1930 specifically linked government subsidy to the number of those displaced and re-housed.

In health care, too, local government acquired additional responsibilities in the interwar period under some 20 Acts of Parliament (Lewis, 1992b, p. 332), while by the 1929 Local Government Act the Poor Law hospitals were transferred to local government control, a move which had 'undoubtedly brought closer the creation of a unified hospital system under public control' (Cole and Cole, 1937, p. 84). The future administration of such a system, however, was a contentious issue. The expansion of the National Health Insurance scheme was advocated by those such as the British Medical Association who were opposed to any increase in the role of local authorities. Health insurance, it has been suggested (Lewis, 1992b, p. 332) represented 'the safest way of broadening service provision without threatening the autonomy and control of the medical profession'. The Socialist Medical Association, however, was an effective publicist both for socialized medicine and for local government control; and during the 1930s 'Labour local authorities worked steadily towards the establishment of comprehensive municipal health services' (Webster, 1988b, p. 198). One of the best-known examples was the London County Council which had created a mini-NHS before the Second World War. Over the country as a whole, however, wide geographical variations persisted, which reflected the financial resources (especially from the local rates) that were available, and there was considerable duplication between the different types of hospital. Jones (1994, p. 78) has suggested that public health policy did not only fail because of lack of coordination or adequate finance. There was, in addition, what she terms 'a fundamental flaw in the ideology behind the policy'. This emphasized individual and personal responsibility and failed to locate the debate about health in the wider socio-economic conditions of the period. It was an issue which historians re-visited in the conditions of large-scale unemployment during the 1980s (for example Whiteside, 1991).

Schooling was another and increasing sector of local government responsibility. In financial terms, the percentage of national income spent by central government remained almost static throughout the interwar period at just over 2 per cent, while local authority expenditure on education increased by 25 per cent. The costs of schooling were thus increasingly borne by local ratepayers. Yet at the same time, central government encouraged the expansion and development of state secondary education, though it offered no financial inducements. The Hadow Report (1926) on *The Education of the Adolescent* established the division between what it thought of as primary and secondary schooling at the age of 11 (making more general the age at which free-place holders and scholarship winners already left the elementary sector) and the separation of the secondary sector into three components. These were subsequently refined by the Spens Report (1938) into grammar, technical and modern schools, thereby establishing the pattern for the form of secondary education implemented after the 1944 Education Act.

Despite the financial constraints, by 1938 almost two-thirds of children were in schools which had reorganized their provision of secondary education for older pupils. There was a significant difference between urban and rural areas however; almost two-thirds of rural school children were still being educated in all-age schools in the late 1930s (Sutherland, 1990, p. 161; Armstrong, 1990, p. 143). Access to selective secondary schooling also fell victim to the economies required of the education budget. The guaranteed 'free places' in the secondary schools were abolished in 1932 – a move which especially hit lower-middle-class families – and replaced by 'special' or means-tested places awarded on the basis of success in a competitive examination. The majority of local authorities also retained a qualifying examination for those whose parents were able to pay the full fee. Though scholarships represented 'a ladder of opportunity' for working-class children, selective secondary schools remained 'the preserve of an elite' with their primacy as 'the route to both respectability and gentility unchallenged' (Sutherland, 1990, p. 162).

During the interwar period the central and local state became more proactively involved in a widening range of welfare activities. This was part of 'the moving frontier' in welfare of the time. In addition, however, there were changes in the relationship between the state and the voluntary sector. Braithwaite's study in the mid-1930s indicated the steadiness of charitable income, despite the effects of economic depression. But her analysis also highlighted changes in the source of such charitable income. The role of individual donations was declining. By contrast, payments by central government or local authorities to the voluntary sector under agency arrangements were increasing significantly. In 1934 Braithwaite estimated that around 37 per cent of the total income of registered charities was being received from the state as payment for services (Braithwaite, 1938, p. 171). This changing relationship between the statutory and voluntary sectors represented a blurring of the public and private and constituted what Elizabeth Macadam (1934) described as 'the new philanthropy'. Finlayson (1990, p. 203) suggested it was a relationship that was beneficial to both parties: to the state 'because even in its more extended form, there was still a desire not to overspend and to use charitable organisations was cheaper than to undertake sole responsibility'; to the voluntary sector 'because there was difficulty in keeping pace with rising costs, and the increasing need to become more professional and to meet more specialised needs' which required resources beyond those on which charities depended.

Not all voluntary agencies welcomed this new relationship, however. Some feared that 'the sector was in danger of losing its independence' (Davis Smith, 1995, p. 26). Others 'shifted their functions into areas where partnership (with the state) was unnecessary' (Prochaska, 1988, p. 80). In the case of the relief of unemployment Harris (1995b, pp. 552–3) has concluded that while 'inter-war governments continued to rely on private charity to fill the gaps in state welfare provision' the voluntary organisations themselves 'devoted an increasing proportion of their time to the development of alternative forms of welfare provision such as educational settlements, unemployed clubs and allotment societies'. In this way, the acceptance of increasing state responsibility for income support, however inadequate it might have been, led to a developing complementarity between public provision and the voluntary sector.

There was less room for manoeuvre in the case of families. Crowther (1982) has suggested that in times of economic stringency there is a tendency for the state to redraw the boundaries so that an increasing responsibility is placed upon families. One of the best-known examples of such a redrawing in the interwar years is the introduction of the household means test in 1931. This involved taking into account the income of other members of the household when assessing the amount of benefit which an unemployed man would receive. This measure not only extended the Poor Law concept of 'liable relatives' to the able-bodied unemployed. It also added, as an additional principle, the notion of mutual financial support between people living in the same household (Finch, 1989, p. 118). In practice, it meant that young working adults living in the same household as their unemployed parents were expected to support them financially. Its effect was to penalize 'the stable families which had remained together' (Crowther, 1982, p. 145), while encouraging young people to leave home to avoid these responsibilities (Finch, 1989, p. 68).

Unemployment and the development of means testing added to the problems of domestic management faced especially by working-class women. One recent summary (D'Cruze, 1995, p. 65) highlights the strategies which they used in order to make ends meet: 'As well as earning income themselves as and when necessary, shopping carefully, economising and sometimes saving, their chief strategies were self-deprivation and the utilisation of the support of children, kin and neighbourhood'. This last, she considers, was the product of 'the local focus of working-class women's lives – that of the neighbourhood and the street' and it provided the means to cope with times of domestic crisis and uncertainty.

It was not only the experience of unemployment that imposed additional responsibilities upon women. The spread of welfare institutions such as child welfare clinics and the increasing public concern with the physical and psychological well-being of children thrust additional responsibilities on to women in relation to child-rearing and development. In the process, they provided an unprecedented surveillance of the working-class population (Donzelot, 1980 Cooter, 1992). Meanwhile, the increasing number of women's magazines that developed in the interwar years strategically shaped 'the cult of domesticity' reinforcing 'the pleasures of home and family life' (Pugh, 1992, pp. 209–10). The surveillance of welfare professionals and the images presented by the popular press thus worked together in the interwar years to heighten the expectations of women as mothers. That too was part of the changing dynamic between the expanding state and family responsibilities.

The interwar years were not only characterized by paradox and policy change. It was also a period in which the notion of planning became a central feature of intellectual discourse and debate. In terms of political activity, planning 'seemed to find its moment in the Second World War' but its antecedents in social and political thought have been traced to before the First World War (Stevenson, 1986, pp. 59–66). In the interwar period, planning was the *leit-motif* of a diversity of quasi-political and intellectual groups, each of whom provided a distinctive gloss to the concept (Ritschl, 1997, *passim*). For some, it was 'a means of refurbishing capitalism', for others 'a means of replacing capitalism by a socialist or corporatist state... But planners were all agreed that market mechanisms could no longer be relied upon to modernise British industry and to lift the economy out of the slump' (Harris, 1990, p. 86). On this issue, there was some political consensus. As Harold Macmillan (1933, p. 18), the Conservative MP and advocate of the 'middle way' expressed it: '"Planning" is forced upon us... not for idealistic reasons but because the old mechanisms which served us when markets were expanding naturally and spontaneously is no longer adequate when the tendency is in the opposite direction'. The Labour politician Ellen Wilkinson (1934, p. 235) expressed a similar view:

> out of the economic storms of our period, one idea is crystallising in the minds of most intelligent people – that planning of some kind has become necessary... No political party could now face the country and say that they proposed to leave economic forces to work themselves out as best they may.

In the short term, the planning movement had little influence on government activity. But it provided a credo around which the dispirited labour movement could re-focus after the ignominious events of 1931. In that context planning was both 'an attractive socialist alternative to the discredited capitalist market system' and 'articulated the desired break with the party's gradualist past and... its new found commitment to a firmly socialist course' (Ritschl, 1997, pp. 99, 100). Labour's *Immediate Programme* of 1937 was the consolidation of that process. It advocated public control of finance, land, transport, coal and power – the principal levers of the economic machine – as well as proposals for higher wages, better pensions, improved education and extended health services (Brooke, 1992, pp. 30–2). When Labour entered the Coalition government in 1940 it did so with a distinctive programme already established in which the notion of planning in the public interest was paramount. Among subsequent historians, this has raised the question of how far the wartime Coalition represented a consensus on domestic issues; and, in view of Labour's policy commitments of the late 1930s, it is perhaps not surprising that they became enthusiastic supporters of the Beveridge Report on its publication in 1942.

Conclusion

By the outbreak of the Second World War, Britain's welfare system remained residual and partial and directed almost exclusively at the working class. This was despite the considerably expanded role both of central and local government in welfare delivery and the changes that had taken place in the boundaries between suppliers in the web of welfare. A decade later the 'classic' welfare state was both more universal in its coverage of the population and more comprehensive in the range of services it provided. How far that represented an evolutionary process from the antecedents that have been reviewed in this chapter and how far it was a revolution created by the special conditions of wartime experience is the theme of the next chapter.

2

CREATION

...a natural development from the past...a British revolution.
(*Social Insurance and Allied Services*, The Beveridge Report, 1942)

The significance of the 1940s in the creation of the 'classic' welfare state can scarcely be over-estimated. It was a decade in which a considerable volume of social legislation passed into law, and when welfare was transformed from a 'demeaning concession to a social right' (Lowe, 1995, p. 372). As the previous chapter has shown, there were many continuities between the legislation of the 1940s and earlier antecedents. But this should not detract from the significance of the 1940s in the creation of a solidaristic welfare state characterized by comprehensiveness and universalism; a creation achieved against daunting postwar economic difficulties. Welfare, which had hitherto been a residual role of government, became institutionalized as one of its legitimate and primary activities. How did this happen? What were the reactions to this process and its impact on other welfare suppliers? To what extent did the creation of the welfare state represent a victory for the vision of a socialist Britain? These are some of the themes to be explored in this chapter.

The Classic Welfare State

The classic welfare state comprised two elements. First was a raft of social legislation passed between 1944 and 1948: the 1944 Education Act, the introduction of family allowances in 1945, the National

Insurance and National Assistance income maintenance programmes which, together with the National Health Service, were inaugurated on 5 July 1948; 'a day' which, as the Labour government publicity campaign proclaimed, 'makes history'. Secondly, there was the commitment to a high and stable level of employment which provided the economic underpinning for the welfare state in general and for maintaining the insurance basis of its social security programme in particular. Together these two elements formed the basis for the recently more contentious notion of the postwar consensus: a closer integration between economic and social policy 'reflecting a fundamental re-ordering of the priorities, responsibilities and boundaries of the state' (Hay, 1996, p. 52).

The Coalition government's White Paper on Employment Policy (1944) was an important factor in that process. With its assertion that postwar governments should seek 'a high and stable level of employment' as one of its primary objectives, it both closed the door on the past and faced a different future. It represented the rejection of the acceptability or inevitability of mass unemployment on the scale experienced between the wars and reflected the growing importance of new economic thinking, best symbolized by Keynes' *General Theory of Employment, Interest and Money* published in 1936. 'Jobs for all, Keynes argued, could only be guaranteed by governments accepting responsibility for the maintenance of domestic demand' (Whiteside, 1995, p. 55). This it could do either indirectly (through redistributive taxation and lower interest rates to stimulate investment) or directly (by public expenditure on capital projects, industrial investment and welfare benefits which would raise working-class consumption). The Employment Policy White Paper incorporated some Keynesian ideas, but historical research has indicated the extent to which the Coalition Government's commitment

> papered over deep differences between the economists of the Economic Section who favoured deficit finance as a solution to unemployment and traditional Treasury officials who stressed the need to pursue rules of public finance which would inhibit ministers from running deficits indefinitely. (Peden, 1991, p. 135)

No legislation ensued from the White Paper and, as Whiteside (1995, p. 56) notes, 'the post-war Labour Government's plans for economic regulation relied more on central state controls than on the use of fiscal and monetary incentives to create jobs'. Compared to rates of unemployment well in excess of 10 per cent throughout the 1930s, however, the average official rate of unemployment was less than 2 per cent between 1945 and 1960. And it has been suggested that the existence of full employment between the mid-1940s and the mid-1970s probably 'did more than any other element in the "post war contract" to change the lives of ordinary people' (Glennerster, 1995a, p. 5).

The Second World War and the Welfare State

We have already seen how the Boer War and the First World War stimulated a concern about social conditions and a greater range of state activity and control over the lives of its citizens. In the opinion of an influential genre of historical writing, the experience of the Second World War produced both 'a swing to the left' politically (Addison, 1975), and created the conditions that facilitated the construction of a solidaristic and universal welfare state. Macnicol (1986, p. 1), himself a critic of such writing, states its position admirably:

> In the social history of twentieth century Britain, the Second World War stands out as a watershed: the sheer scale and magnitude of the events that took place during those crucial six years seems to lend indisputable credibility to the view that modern wars are a major force behind progressive social change.

That interpretation was crucial to Richard Titmuss's account in the volume on social policy which he wrote for the official *History of the Second World War*. 'Out of an analysis of the policies for war time evacuation, the care of the homeless and the emergency hospital service Timuss had produced', according to one assessment (Gowing, 1975, p. 13) 'a profound work of history, of the study of society'. Titmuss's account indicated how:

> The German bomber offensive forced public authorities to set up an emergency hospital service, to provide communal feeding arrangements, to requisition surplus housing, to organise mass evacuation and to provide foster homes for millions of urban children. (Harris, 1990, p. 90)

The consequence was not only a proliferation of public social services. Its impact was more far-reaching, encompassing,

> a revolution in popular expectations about the role of the state. Government was seen no longer merely as the guarantor of private freedom and the prop of the very poor: 'instead it was increasingly regarded as a proper function or even obligation of government to ward off distress and strain among not only the poor but almost all classes of society... the mood of the people changed and in sympathetic response values changed as well'. (*ibid.*)

More recent historical research has developed a significant critique of the Titmuss thesis. It has questioned, first, his interpretation of wartime solidarity. Wartime experiences such as the rationing of food and clothing and indiscriminate bombing 'may have democratised hardship, fostering a greater sense of social cohesion... but the strength of class attitudes and the existence of social divisions should not be under estimated' (Digby, 1989, pp. 54–5). There was a world of difference between those dining in well-known London hotels and restaurants, and the population seeking refuge in its underground stations. Similarly, the existence of a vigorous wartime black market casts doubt on the solidarity that Titmuss detected (Dewey, 1997, p. 316). Nor it seems did the process of evacuation of women and children from urban to rural areas, which was central to Titmuss's thesis, provide an unequivocal shock to public consciousness and a new commitment to right the interwar experiences of children reared amid conditions of financial poverty, ill-health and unemployment. A more recent assessment (Calder, 1991, p. 63) has concluded that 'heightened social awareness among some sections of the middle class clearly did not exclude the sharpening of prejudice in others'.

Secondly, more recent writing has emphasized continuities between the legislation of the 1940s and its earlier antecedents, as well as in public attitudes:

> Almost all the ideas and proposals for reform in social security and education, for example, had long been discussed in the 1920s and 1930s. The new structures built on or simplified many of the systems that preceded them. In many cases they extended to a national scale experiments which had been introduced by some local authorities. (Glennerster, 1990, p. 11)

Meanwhile Harris's (1983b) re-working of data from G.D.H. Cole's Reconstruction Survey has led her to question whether the attitudes towards welfare of the British working class changed as significantly as Titmuss argued:

> In general the tenor of the evidence was more modest and less ambitious than that of the reforms proposed later in 1942 in the Beveridge Plan. 'More of the same' rather than radical change was the wish of most respondents. (p. 294)

Thirdly in their attempt to account for the creation of the classic welfare state, recent writers have suggested other factors than those which Titmuss identified and a complex patterning between them. One of these concerns political activity. '... by inviting the Labour and Liberal parties to join the Coalition, Churchill broke the Conservative political hegemony of the inter-war years' (Kavanagh and Morris, 1989, p. 16). It is generally agreed that while Churchill devoted himself to war objectives, matters of domestic policy were left in the hands of Labour members of the Coalition, with Attlee as Deputy Prime Minister. That – and their perceived warmer welcome for the Beveridge proposals – may help to explain Labour's election victory in 1945 (Jefferys, 1987, p. 130). The Conservatives loss of power has also been attributed to their internal ideological divisions and a greatly weakened party machine (Ramsden, 1995, Ch. 2). But Churchill himself, although apparently less interested in domestic affairs, unwittingly gave shape to the ideology of reform. In nationalistic terms Churchill's rhetoric emphasized 'a common people united in a common cause'; their shared determination to win the war. 'No longer were the British workers seen as the idle, intractable, trouble makers of previous years'. As soldiers and citizens they were 'called to the centre of the national stage ... in a patriotic struggle for justice, liberty, equality against oppression' (Morgan and Evans, 1993, p. 21). In that sense the people's war necessitated the people's peace. But unlike the aftermath of the First World War, 'this time ... the past would be exorcised and the future transformed' (Morgan, 1990, p. 4).

Planning

A greater degree of centralized planning was to be the means of achieving that future transformation. As the previous chapter has

indicated, the notion of planning was already in vogue. It had become
the centrepiece of informed, progressive opinion during the 1930s
(Marwick, 1963; Ritschl, 1997). But it was the exigencies of war that
legitimized an increasing control over the lives of British citizens. That
control applied not only in the theatres of war. There was also extensive
central government planning and direction that applied to civilians: the
evacuation of women and schoolchildren from urban to rural areas;
the inception of the Emergency Medical Service to deal with wartime
casualties; the rationing of food and clothing and other essential
supplies; the direction of labour, and the scheme to deal with bombed-
out houses and homeless families. Commenting on the Emergency
Powers Act which passed through Parliament in a single day in 1940,
one of the official historians of the Second World War pointed out that

> In a matter of three hours the traditional liberty of British citizens to
> manage their own lives and property was, by the free vote of the
> Parliamentary representatives, surrendered for the duration of the
> war to the will of a government statutorily vested with arbitrary
> powers of direction. (Parker, 1957, p. 95)

Wartime conditions may have facilitated and legitimised a more proactive and directing role for government, but another link exists between
the interwar planning movement and the legislation of the 1940s. It is
supplied by those academics and opinion-formers of the 1930s who were
recruited into government and the civil service during the war. Ritschl
(1997, p. 207) has argued that 'the existence of a cohesive progressive
Keynesian establishment' is a 'highly tendentious notion', and has suggested that social reconstruction was a more complex process of negotiation and compromise. Even accepting that interpretation, however, it
is still important to recognize the transformation which the civil service
underwent during the war. Not only did the number of those in the
highest grades more than double during that time, many temporary
staff were also recruited from the universities. In that new milieu, 'very
often it was people that mattered – individuals or small groups that
really counted in shifting a policy blockage' (Hennessy, 1993, p. 43).
Meanwhile, as a consequence of its changing personnel, Addison (1987,
p. 11) has suggested that 'postwar planning acquired an institutional
momentum that was practically irreversible by 1945'.

Whether as an ideology or a pragmatic activity of government, planning was not universally popular. Until the publication of Hayek's *Road*

to Serfdom in 1944, however, opposition was diffuse among back-bench Conservative MPs, the Aims of Industry and the Society of Individualists founded by Sir Ernest Benn. Hayek's purpose was to provide a heightened public awareness and critical assessment of 'the main principles of "planning" that were [by then] largely taken for granted behind the closed doors of Whitehall' (Cockett, 1995, p. 79). Dedicated to 'the Socialists of all Parties', *The Road to Serfdom* provided a 'vigorous and articulate restatement of the libertarian anti-statist case' (Barker, 1997, p. 144). In it, Hayek argued that because of its arbitrary nature, planning led inevitably to tyranny and corruption, even in the hands of the most well-meaning administrators. Hence *The Road to Serfdom* of his title. 'The important thing now', he opined, 'is that we...free ourselves from some of the errors that have governed us in the recent past...The guiding principle, that a policy of freedom for the individual is the only true progressive policy, remains as true today as it was in the nineteenth century' (Hayek, 1944, pp. 177–8). The then Conservative Party Chairman Ralph Assheton ordered several copies of Hayek's book to send to leading colleagues, and it has been suggested (Jones, 1992, pp. 105–8) that it was through him that 'Hayekian rhetoric' entered Churchill's language in 1945. It would recur thirty years later with the election of Margaret Thatcher as leader of the Conservative Party.

Wartime experience and the planning movement's commitment to administrative rationalization came together in the Beveridge Report.

The Beveridge Report, 1942

At the time of its publication in December 1942 the Report by Sir William Beveridge was an instant best-seller. Its title – *Social Insurance and Allied Services* – might have suggested otherwise; so too might the fact that it represented the work of an inter-departmental committee of middle-ranking civil servants whose remit from Arthur Greenwood, the Minister without Portfolio in the Coalition government was

> to undertake, with special reference to the interrelation of the schemes, a survey of the existing national schemes of social insurance and allied services, including workmen's compensation and to make recommendations. (Cmd. 6404, p. 2)

Nor was it initially the task that Beveridge wanted. As Master of University College, Oxford he had been drafted into the wartime Ministry of Labour to provide specialist advice on manpower and labour questions, on which his reputation had already been established before the First World War. In the event, Beveridge accepted the job, was the sole signatory of the final Report and proposed a blue-print for change that went far beyond its initial remit. In that lay its popular appeal. 'There has never been an official report like it' (Hennessy, 1993, p. 73).

Ostensibly it was a technocratic document: a contribution to the greater rationalization and administrative organization of the income maintenance system. But it was more, because of its identification of social insurance as

> one part only of a comprehensive policy of social progress. Social insurance fully developed may provide income security, it is an attack upon Want. But Want is only one of the five giants on the road to reconstruction. The others are Disease, Ignorance, Squalor and Idleness. (Cmd. 6404, para. 8)

Published shortly after the British success at the Battle of Alamein, when for the first time in the Second World War ultimate victory seemed possible, the comprehensive vision of social progress offered by the Beveridge Report 'was seen by many people as the light at the end of the tunnel of war, and as a promise of "social justice" for the post-war world' (Harris, 1977, p. 1). In the short term 'support for the Beveridge Plan became an earnest of political good intentions' (Silburn, 1995, p. 93). It put pressure on the Coalition government 'to give serious – rather than token – attention to the problems of reconstruction', but at the same time it 'brought to the surface and pinpointed the tensions of Coalition politics' (Jefferys, 1991, pp. 118–19). The Labour Party gave a warmer welcome to the Beveridge proposals than did the Conservatives. In his study of the Labour Party during the Second World War, Brooke highlighted the parallels between Beveridge's rhetoric and Labour policy as well as the widespread support for the Report across all sections of the Labour movement. As a result, he concludes, 'the Beveridge Report...became an icon for the labour movement' (Brooke, 1992, p. 166).

Meanwhile, the Conservatives were more divided and lukewarm in their response. There were those Conservatives who had been associated with the interwar planning movement and 'the middle way' who were more positive about the Beveridge proposals (Charmley, 1996, p. 113). On the other hand, there were those who argued that his scheme threatened both the importance of reducing wartime levels of taxation and the ethos of individual initiative and self-reliance. For Churchill himself 'the implementation of post-war reforms would have to depend upon the state of the economy and the Government's ability to pay for them' (Addison, 1993, p. 358). As a result 'Labour became identified with and committed to a programme which may have arisen from a very different political quarter but which they soon made their own' (Cronin, 1991, p. 139). In Fielding's (1992, pp. 633–4) vivid expression, 'If the Conservatives had previously won votes by wrapping themselves in the flag, after 1942 Labour covered itself with the pages of the Beveridge Report'. That identification would prove particularly significant at the time of the 1945 general election:

> when with both Labour and Conservatives pledging a comprehensive system of social insurance and a national health service along Beveridge lines, the issue turned on which party could best be trusted to convert fine words into reality. (Hennessy, 1993, p. 77)

labour ⱽ conservative who could make the report happen

The 1945 General Election

The general election of 1945 was the first to be held for ten years. It produced the first majority Labour government in British history, with 393 seats compared to the Conservatives' 210 and an overall Labour majority of 146 MPs. In the election Labour obtained a virtual monopoly of working-class votes for the first time, while almost one-quarter of the middle class voted Labour (Bonham, 1954, pp. 129–30). This 'gave the party the edge over the Conservatives in a host of metroland constituencies' (Fielding, 1992, p. 637). Nationally, of the 209 net gains made by Labour, 79 were in constituencies which had never before returned a Labour member (McCallum and Readman, 1947, p. 261). Searching for historical parallels, the Nuffield election study placed the 1945 election alongside those of 1832 and 1906 (*ibid*., p. 247).

The Labour manifesto was both backward and forward looking. It summoned up the image of the hard-faced men of business who, after the First World War, 'were able to get the kind of peace that suited themselves' (Craig, 1975, p. 123), and warned against the anti-controllers and anti-planners [who] desire to sweep away public controls simply in order to give the profiteering interests and privileged rich an entirely free hand to plunder the rest of the nation as shamelessly as they did in the nineteen twenties. (*ibid.*, p. 24)

Labour's appeal to 'men and women of progressive outlook...who believe in constructive change' was in terms of its domestic programme: its policies for full employment and public ownership of basic industries and its commitments on house building, education, health and social insurance. Especially on these welfare issues, the Labour Party was well aware of the need to break with the wartime consensus, though as recent research has indicated that consensus may have been more apparent than real. 'All parties may declare that in principle they agree with them. But the test of a political programme is whether it is sufficiently earnest about the objectives to adopt the means needed to realise them' (*ibid.*, p. 124).

Viewed historically, Labour's victory has been attributed to the steady momentum building during the 1940s. Addison (1975, p. 14) emphasized the 'swing to the left' creating in the process a new consensus 'that fell like a branch of ripe plums into the lap of Mr. Attlee'. Pelling (1980, p. 411) similarly identified a 'steady strengthening of left wing feeling', an interpretation borne out by the results of Gallup poll surveys which showed Labour with a steady lead over the Conservatives from 1943. Though the gap between the parties had narrowed by the eve of the election, Ramsden (1995, p. 89) considers that for the Conservatives 'defeat probably was inescapable in 1945' arguing that the recovery that had taken place 'was in spite of rather than because of the Party's national election campaign'. For the Labour Party its election victory represented a significant turnaround in its fortunes after the barren decade of the 1930s; an entry into the inheritance 'bequeathed them by the pioneers of the party and the founding fathers' (Morgan, 1984, p. 7). 'All agreed', James Chuter Ede, the Labour Home Secretary, remarked, 'that the results surpassed our wildest dreams' (cited Brooke, 1992, p. 1), while Hugh Dalton (1962, p. 3), his colleague as Chancellor of the Exchequer, felt he was 'walking on air, walking with destiny'. Once in government Labour 'presents a picture both of continuity and departure' (Brooke, 1992, p. 329) in developing its welfare programme. It is to elements of that programme that we now turn.

Labour's Welfare Programme

Labour's social programme has received considerable attention from historians. It has been variously described as 'a mosaic of reform and conservatism' (Morgan, 1984, p. 179) and the implementation of 'practical socialism' which none the less remained 'a radical programme' (Brooke, 1992, p. 315). More recently, in challenging the notion of postwar consensus, Francis (1996b, p. 54) has included the welfare sector as one of the areas where 'the Attlee government invested its policies with a specifically socialist character'.

The Labour government inherited two measures of social reform – the Education Act and the Family Allowances Act – which had been passed in 1944 and 1945. Family allowances were one of three assumptions on which Beveridge based his plan for social security. In advocating their introduction, Beveridge became a party to a long-standing campaign which is especially associated with Eleanor Rathbone. As Land (1975) and Macnicol (1980) have argued, however, the family allowances legislation owed less to a concern with mothers and children than as a solution to the issue of wartime pay and allowances. 'It was only when family allowances were proffered as a means of non-statutory, non-inflationary pay limitation that their attraction as a universal benefit became apparent' (Vincent, 1991, pp. 116–17). While welcoming their introduction, Eleanor Rathbone herself deplored both the amount to be paid – 5 shillings (25p) for second and subsequent children, which was 3 shillings (15p) less than Beveridge had proposed, and the fact that they were to be paid to men (Alberti, 1996, p. 141).

The second measure inherited by the Labour government was the 1944 Education Act, the result of a constructive partnership between R.A. Butler (Conservative) and James Chuter Ede (Labour) his deputy at the Board of Education. That Act had made secondary education available to all by the abolition of fees and introduced a progressive staging of schooling with the break between primary and secondary education occurring at the age of 11-plus. The Act did not specify the form of secondary education, though it was implicit from the recommendations of the Spens (1938) and Norwood (1943) Reports that it would be organized on tripartite lines into grammar, technical and secondary-modern schools. 'What the 1944 settlement achieved was a rationalisation and an expansion of *existing* patterns of educational provision' (Hennessy, 1993, p. 155). It was a settlement which turned out to be safe in Labour's hands.

School   family Allowance.

This has led some to criticize the Attlee government for its failure to introduce a distinctively socialist policy in the field of education (see Rubinstein, 1979; Benn, 1980). On the other hand, various factors have been put forward to account for Labour's continuing commitment to the 1944 settlement. One of these concerns the other demands faced by the Labour Ministry of Education: for replacing school buildings, increasing the supply of teachers, responding to the increased birth rate – between 1942 and the end of 1947 a million more children were born than in the previous five years – and the commitment to raising the school leaving age to 15 in 1947. Another sees the support for grammar schools as a product of the personal experience of Ellen Wilkinson, Labour's first Minister of Education, for whom such a school had been both a means of her intellectual enrichment and of her advancement to Manchester University (Vernon, 1982). Through the abolition of fees such opportunities were now more widely available as a means of self-improvement to the hard-working and intelligent children of working-class families.

Such support, however, was at variance with the critique of the tripartite system offered by the National Association of Labour Teachers and its commitment to multilateral schools (an early version of comprehensive education). Only such schools, according to Benn and Rubinstein, constitute a distinctively socialist approach to education. Francis (1997), however, has argued that such a view was very much a minority opinion in the 1940s Labour Party, despite the adoption of a resolution supporting the multilateral school at the 1942 Labour Party conference. Francis shows how other educational organizations within the Party supported tripartism, while few Labour-controlled local authorities submitted plans for educational reorganization along comprehensive lines. For most sections of the Labour Party in the 1940s, therefore, he suggests, free secondary education and equality of educational opportunity rather than common schools for all 'were felt to be fundamental tenets of progressive educational policy' (ibid., p. 149).

That stance was already changing as Labour left government in 1951; but during its period in power it had presided over a 'a massive expansion of secondary schooling which in practice confirmed the distinctions in an already divided educational system' (Roy Lowe, 1988, p. 53).

In the aftermath of wartime bombing and destruction, housing was an important public issue. Labour's commitment at the time of the 1945 general election was to 'proceed with a housing programme with the maximum practical speed until every family in this land has a good

housing

standard of accommodation' (cited in Craig, 1975, p. 129). Much has been made of the obstacles that potentially prevented Labour from achieving that objective: the shortage of raw materials, competition for labour and materials from other sectors where postwar rebuilding was necessary, financial constraint and organizational bureaucracy. It is perhaps the more surprising, therefore, that by the end of Labour's term in office in 1951, more than one million permanent homes had been built, though 'the totals were relatively disappointing since lengthy waiting lists remained' (Addison, 1985, p. 69).

Much has also been made of the ideological divide between the Labour government and the Conservative opposition, the former supporting council-house building, the latter, the removal of controls on private builders. Bevan's apparent doctrinaire preference for council housing has recently been questioned (Francis, 1997, p. 118), but the same author has also argued that Labour's public housing programmes was 'invested with a specifically socialist content' both in its allocation on the basis of housing need and the improved standards of quality which Bevan introduced (*ibid.*, p. 129). 'Determined to level the working classes up, he opted for standards that were ambitious in the context of austerity' (Addison, 1985, p. 70). That led to criticism, not least from within his own party, that the sacrifice of quantity to quality was a mistake. The Conservatives reversed those priorities on their return to power in 1951.

Bevan is principally remembered, however, not so much for his work on housing as for his role in the creation of the National Health Service (the two responsibilities were combined in his Ministry of Health). Its principal features had been foreshadowed in the Coalition government's White Paper on *A National Health Service* which proposed that such a service should be comprehensive and free to the user at the point of demand. But there was a longer antecedent history. The Webb's Minority Report to the Poor Law Commission in 1909 had suggested the creation of a public or state medical service, and the creation of a National Health Service was one of the assumptions on which Beveridge based his plan for social security. For Beveridge, access to speedy diagnosis, treatment and rehabilitation was essential in order to ensure that employees returned to work as quickly as possible. In that way, demand on the social security system would be kept in check. The Socialist Medical Association meanwhile had its advocacy of a comprehensive state health service endorsed as Labour Party policy in the 1930s; and, with the creation of the Emergency Hospital Service to deal with wartime casualties, a prototype state-funded hospital service supervised by the Ministry of Health was already in operation.

A substantial literature exists which portrays the creation of the NHS as a measure of consensus and compromise. As a measure of consensus it is depicted as the natural successor of the 1944 White Paper and the result of civil servants and representatives of medical interest groups 'searching out the limits of the acceptable' (Klein, 1995, p. 10). More recent studies, however, have revealed 'an increasing level of controversy beneath the surface of party agreement' (Jefferys, 1991, p. 130) and have highlighted the distinctive nature of Labour's contribution to the post-war NHS (for example Webster, 1988b,) That contribution, however, was worked out in government in the face of considerable opposition from the medical profession (especially the general practitioners) whose support was crucial to the working of any health care scheme. Much of the political controversy between 1946 and the inauguration of the NHS on the appointed day 5 July 1948 centred on their concerns and fears. The compromises that resulted, it has been suggested, meant that the NHS although ostensibly presented as a socialist measure 'in reality...had become the captive of corporate interest' (Webster, 1988b, p. 199). The concessions included capitation fees instead of a state-salaried medical service, retaining pay beds in NHS hospitals and the system of private practice.

Administratively, the structure preserved the long-standing divisions in British medicine, while Bevan also failed 'to promote the cause of the local health centre which promised to substitute co-operation for competition between doctors' (Francis, 1997, p. 102). Setting these concessions alongside the commitments of Labour's 1943 policy document *National Service for Health*, some have challenged the socialist character of the NHS that was eventually created (see Powell, 1997, pp. 44–53). Francis (1997, p. 102), however, has argued that despite the concessions, 'the new service still successfully satisfied a number of socialist maxims'. One of these was the introduction of comprehensive coverage. Others included, 'a nationalisation of the hospital services, the allocation of resources according to need rather that the vagaries of the market, the abolition of the sale of practices, the principle of free access and a degree of redistribution between income groups'. To the population then – and subsequently – however, the NHS represented 'the jewel in the crown' of Britain's welfare state. Politically it was 'a unique experiment in social engineering' and 'the first health system in any Western society to offer free medical care to the whole population' (Klein, 1995, vii, p. 1).

It was not only the NHS which was inaugurated on 5 July 1948. That date also saw the introduction of the Labour government's measures of income security through National Insurance and National Assistance. The National Insurance Act 1946 provided a more comprehensive set of benefits to a wider section of the population and took their administration away from the Friendly Societies by making it a direct responsibility of the Ministry of National Insurance. There was considerable cross-party unanimity. Opposition from Labour dissidents centred around two principal issues: the variety of qualifications imposed on the payment of benefits and the actual amounts to be paid which, in some cases, were lower than Beveridge had recommended (Morgan, 1984, p. 172).

Labour's 1948 National Assistance Act, however, represented a more significant break with Beveridge's proposals. Whereas he had advocated a unified Ministry of Social Security, National Assistance was to be administered separately from the insurance benefit system through the quasi-autonomous National Assistance Board. And whereas Beveridge had envisaged a residual role for a small declining number of claimants in any means-tested system, in fact it assumed an increasing importance against the giant Want. The reasons for this are complex (Deacon, 1982); but they centre on the fact that contributory benefits were fixed at levels that were not sufficient for subsistence. In addition, while assistance benefits included an allowance for rent, insurance benefits did not. These factors were compounded by an inconsistent pattern of up-rating for the two types of benefit. As a result 'means tested benefits which Beveridge had hoped would wither away expanded both to "top up" inadequate insurance benefits and to support the uninsured' (Lowe, 1994, p. 363). Labour's social security measures represented a closer approximation to the introduction of a national minimum than any previous government action (Thane, 1996, p. 238) but the means test remained as a continuing and expanding feature of Britain's income maintenance system.

Reacting to the Welfare State

By the legislative programme enacted between 1945 and 1951 'government had accepted unprecedented responsibility for economic stability and social welfare...All of this was a far cry from *laissez-faire* principles, even if the principle of "less eligibility" remained enshrined in the operation of the National Assistance Board' (Peden, 1991, p. 151). How far it represented a distinctively socialist programme, however, remains an open question, as recent studies of particular facets of Labour's programme have suggested.

What then of reactions to Labour's creation of the classic welfare state? Earlier in this chapter we noted both the public enthusiasm and professional opposition for the NHS, the political criticism of elements of the social security legislation highlighted by some of Labour's own MPs, and Hayek's more sustained theoretical critique of collectivist planning. Beveridge too, as his biographer tells us, disliked the term 'welfare state' preferring '"social service state" which implied that citizens had duties as well as rights' (Harris, 1977, p. 459). This section focuses on two elements of reaction and response: the political response of the Conservative opposition and the impact upon other welfare sectors of the growing role of the state.

One established tradition of historical writing suggests that the Conservative Party progressively came to terms with the welfare state, an accommodation that laid the foundations for a Keynesian–Beveridge consensus in matters of economic and social policy. More recent studies, by contrast, have emphasized the differences that existed between the partners in the Coalition government and the distinctly different ideological perspectives of the Conservative and Labour parties between 1945 and 1951.

Writing of the wartime coalition, Brooke (1992, p. 170) suggests that even on those measures evincing the most agreement – such as the 1944 Education Act and the Employment Policy White Paper – 'there remained a profound difference between the Conservative and Labour parties'. Kandiah (1996, pp. 58–78), meanwhile, is among those who have drawn attention to the distinctive characteristics of the Conservative Party platform in 1945. These he describes as 'anti-statism, the preservation of capitalism (though not necessarily all-out *laissez-faire* capitalism), limited reform and the belief in individual freedoms and opportunity'. It was these, he suggests, that were the 'broad parameters' within which the Party leaders were to operate in subsequent years' (*ibid.*, p. 59). In consequence,

Conservative leaders did not share the assumptions which underpinned Labour's vision of post-war Britain; they were determined to construct and then maintain Conservatism as a distinct and viable alternative to Labour's socialism. (*ibid.*, p. 74)

This distinctive ethos was reflected not only in the Conservative equation of socialism with continuing wartime austerity and controls (Zweiniger-Bargielowska, 1994) but also in its rethinking after the 1945 election defeat. Several writers (for example Charmley, 1996, p. 125; Francis, 1996a, p. 64) have discussed the tensions between the paternalist and libertarian strands in the Conservatism of the time, but in the context of the welfare state 'the cost, the way it was being financed and the form it was taking were all offensive to the liberal view of the state that became the basis of Conservative philosophy' in the later 1940s (Glennerster, 1995a, p. 73). This manifested itself in a variety of ways: in support for free market enterprise (as in housing construction, for example), cuts in public spending, individual initiative in a property-owning democracy, and an increasingly targeted welfare state. As Kandiah (1996, p. 59) critically observes, the '"New Conservatism" would appear to be not too far removed from "Old Conservatism"'.

Conservative politicians were among those who feared that the welfare state would undermine the responsibilities of family life. Means and Smith (1985) have suggested that this view had widespread publicity especially in relation to the care of elderly relatives. Though it was less prevalent among Labour politicians, it also received considerable professional legitimacy. 'The great fear was that the wider availability of domiciliary care would be used by carers to abandon elderly relatives to the state' (Means, 1995, p. 202). Although it was not stated explicitly, the underlying assumption 'was that it should be the responsibility of women to stay at home and look after dependent people' (Finch, 1989, p. 128). In this way, it becomes possible to explain the tardy development of personal welfare services within the welfare state.

A similar case can be made in respect of children. When the war ended, 'the politicians and professionals who stressed the importance of rebuilding the family also stressed the importance of full-time motherhood' (Lewis, 1992a, p. 71). In fact, there were 'mixed messages' from within the postwar Labour government. The Ministries of Health and Education supported the notion of full-time motherhood. Faced with a labour shortage, the Ministry of Labour by contrast began to encourage the combination of domestic responsibilities with part-time employment. Contemporary child care experts, such as Winnicott and Bowlby, however, reinforced the importance of full-time motherhood. One recent assessment has concluded that Bowlby's work became extraordinarily influential in the postwar world 'mainly because it could be used by the government in its pro-natalist attempts to reconstruct family life' (Hendrick, 1997, p. 32). Despite the alarms about the loss of family responsibility consequent on the creation of the welfare state, the research evidence of this period and beyond showed the persistence of family-based care, much of it supplied by women.

Another and related issue concerns the impact of a more comprehensive supply of state welfare on the voluntary sector. The traditional view is that it declined both in influence and supply of services. There is certainly much to support that interpretation: the majority of hospitals were taken into state ownership, while the Friendly Societies lost their role to the civil servants of the Ministry of National Insurance; the voluntary sector found it difficult to compete as an employer, and there were fears that, with a more comprehensive welfare state, voluntary funds would dry up. It 'must have felt like the writing on the wall for many voluntary organisations that had been major providers in the past' (Taylor, 1995, p. 219).

A more recent view argues that 'the Labour Party and its leaders were far less statist in their attitude towards welfare reform than has sometimes been suggested (Deakin, 1995, p. 40). It did not follow, however, that they had altogether abandoned their dislike of the 'do good' volunteer. This too was an area of 'mixed messages' in the postwar Labour government. For Attlee the voluntary sector was integral to democratic citizenship, while Morrison sought a greater cooperation between statutory and voluntary welfare. There were others, however, such as Crossman (1976) who wanted to see the volunteer 'replaced by professional and trained administrators in the socialist welfare state of which we all dreamed'. In practical terms, there can be little doubt that the sphere of the voluntary sector declined as a consequence of Labour's legislative programme. Underpinning that programme was the perception that

The more importance attached to the need for universal provision, for basic guaranteed levels of service and for legally established rights... the more likely the service was to be taken into the public sector entirely. (Brenton, 1985, p. 18)

Personal welfare was an exception to these principles. As a result, the voluntary sector retained a continuing presence in the welfare state especially among elderly people and in leisure and youth services, often acting as an agent for the relevant local government departments.

Readjustment was also a feature of the relations between the commercial sector and the state. Here, too, there is evidence of the Labour government's 'mixed messages', and the contrast between education, housing and income maintenance is instructive.

At the time of the 1944 Education Act the issue of private, fee-paying schools was largely left off the agenda because the Fleming Committee had not reported. Throughout its period in government Labour failed to address the issue; a failure which has been attributed to the fear of public criticism and the indifference of members of its own party (Francis, 1997, pp. 160, 163). Though it has been suggested that conditions at the time were propitious for action on private education (Timmins, 1995, pp. 86–7), Labour's programme maintained the *status quo ante bellum*.

Housing presents a rather different picture. Despite the view cited earlier that Bevan was not ideologically opposed to the private sector, his commitment in his housing programme was principally to the public rather than the private sector. For Bevan, this was 'not merely a short-term necessity but a long-term instrument in the achievement of social-ism' (Jones, 1992, p. 131). Accordingly, private builders were initially limited to one licence for every four that were issued, with additional controls imposed on those licences that were issued to the private sector (Morgan, 1984, p. 164). Not surprisingly, housing was one of the sectors where Conservative opposition was most pronounced during Labour's period in office. Initially they opposed the degree of public intervention in Labour's programme, and later in the 1940s were able to highlight its failure to deliver. That failure was also 'the failure of socialism to deliver what free enterprise had done efficiently before the war' (Jones, 1992, p. 132) and as such played a part in the reconstruction of the Conservat-ive Party itself after its defeat in 1945.

With its guarantee of more comprehensive social security payments against the risks of ill-health, unemployment and old age, Labour's legislation also potentially threatened the commercial insurance compan-ies. As Hannah (1986, p. 44) notes, especially in the context of retire-ment pensions, 'insurance companies feared that their market for pensions sales would cease to expand in the post-war climate'. That concern was short-lived. By the mid-1950s the tax advantages from private pensions were already well-established (*ibid.*, p. 55). Meanwhile, there was also a considerable expansion in company welfare schemes after 1945 covering sickness, accident and pensions. Their extent led Townsend (1976, p. 261) to consider the 'term "fringe benefits" inap-propriate'.

They were also highlighted in Titmuss's seminal essay *The Social Division of Welfare* (1963). In it he argued that the public supply of welfare was only one facet of the contemporary social division of welfare. Occupational welfare schemes and fiscal welfare via tax arrangements and relief represented its other dimensions. And by favouring the better off, they called into question the solidaristic principles of what was conventionally thought of as the welfare state.

Conclusion

Compared with what had preceded it, the welfare legislation of the 1940s represented a considerable extension of state responsibility, whose shape owed much to earlier developments as well as to the specific conditions of the 1940s, both during and after the war. To contemporaries 'there was a widespread belief that the new social services, combined with high levels of income tax and death duties, were rapidly leading to a more equal and integrated society' (Harris, 1990, p. 103). In retrospect, the principal significance of the decade reviewed in this chapter lies in the changing balance between the state and other suppliers in the mixed economy of welfare. But what shape would the welfare state, established in conditions of wartime austerity, take in the next and more affluent quarter century? It is to that period that we now turn.

3

CONSENSUS?

Consensus: agreement (of opinion, testimony); majority view.
(Concise Oxford Dictionary)

The Conservative Party led by Winston Churchill was returned to government in 1951. It continued in power under the successive leadership of Eden, Macmillan and Douglas-Home until 1964. Six years of Labour government followed with Harold Wilson as Prime Minister. The surprise victory of Edward Heath at the 1970 general election brought the Conservatives back to power until 1974 when the Labour government of Harold Wilson and subsequently James Callaghan remained in office until 1979. Conservatives were thus in power for twice the period of Labour governments in the quarter century covered by this chapter.

For many historians and contemporaries, however, it mattered little which political party was in power. For them the period is one of consensus and a strong bi-partisan political commitment to uphold the essential features of the postwar settlement. Writing in the mid-1960s, T. H. Marshall (1975 edition, p. 97) suggested that there was now 'little difference of opinion as to the services that must be provided, and it is generally agreed that, whoever provided them, the overall responsibility for the welfare of its citizens must rest with the state'. For Mishra, (1984, p. 1) the social welfare settlement 'seemed so integral to post-war society as to be almost irreversible'. Welfare, it seemed, was part of the middle ground of postwar politics and where disputed issues arose they were questions about means rather than ends. This was 'the end of ideology' discussed by Daniel Bell in 1960. 'There is today', he affirmed,

'a rough consensus among intellectuals on political issues: the acceptance of a welfare state...a system of mixed economy and political
pluralism' (1960, p. 373).

The argument for consensus appears to have much to commend it.
Despite the fears of their Labour opponents, on their return to government the Conservatives did not dismantle the welfare state of the 1940s.
By 1951 one assessment concludes 'the party had in effect accepted the
verdict of the 1945 electorate and the idea of a welfare state. It had little
enthusiasm for the structure Labour had erected, but it had no inten-
tion of dismantling it either' (Turner, 1996, p. 318). There was also a
strong personal commitment to 'the middle way' during the premiership of Harold Macmillan (1957–63). In addition, both parties were
increasingly concerned to win the support of the 'floating voter' whose
role in determining the outcome of elections was seen to be especially
important.

Consequently, 'the Conservative and Labour parties were compelled
electorally to tone down their ideological commitment and rhetoric in
order to "capture" the middle ground and hence woo the "floating
voters" deemed to be occupying that territory' (Dorey, 1996, p. 61).
The argument in favour of consensus is also strengthened by the commitment of governments of whatever political complexion to maximize the
efficiency, effectiveness and availability of public services. The reform of
the National Health Service which covered both Labour and Conservative governments between 1967 and 1974 is a good case in point.

Consensus, however, has become a contested concept. Pimlott (1988)
has suggested that it may not so much describe as distort a period of
Britain's recent past. For him, the term has ideological rather than
descriptive significance. 'Especially since Mrs Thatcher took office in
1979 and began to introduce major changes, the view has gained wide
acceptance that British politics used to be characterised by a consensus,
but that this nation-uniting mood no longer exists' (ibid., p. 129). As
an ideological device, Pimlott suggested, consensus had an appeal to
both the political Left and Right. To those on the Left it represented
a lost golden age that had been replaced by ideological politics,
monetarism and privatization; the antithesis of what they saw as the
essentials of the postwar settlement. For the political Right during
Mrs Thatcher's period as Prime Minister (1979–90) it symbolized a
period from which they desired to break free into a new style of leadership and a more radical programme. 'Mrs Thatcher, it is argued, turned
back the collectivist tide and thus restored "true" Conservative values

after the compromises, muddle and defeatism of the consensus years' (Charmley, 1996, p. 146).

Just as historians have recently questioned the consensus of wartime Coalition politics, they have also highlighted the differences between the political parties in the period covered by this chapter. Such a view was cogently expressed by the Labour politician Anthony Crosland (1962, p. 123) who suggested that

> deep differences exist between the two parties about the priority to be accorded to social welfare. This is not because Conservatives are less humanitarian, but because they hold particular views as to the proper role of the State, the desirable level of taxation and the importance of private as opposed to collective responsibility. Their willingness for social expenditure is circumscribed by these views and the consequence is a quite different order of priorities.

What this difference in priorities represented has been described by Lowe (1993, p. 85):

> Labour's priority was to engineer a more equal society through greater state intervention and, if necessary, higher taxation; the Conservatives were willing only to accept that degree of intervention and taxation which was compatible with market efficiency and personal initiative.

Over the 30-year period from 1945, there is much evidence which supports the existence of interparty differences on issues of taxation, public spending and the principles that should govern the supply of services. That, however, is not to say that these differences persisted over the whole period or that they applied to all sectors of welfare. The 1960s, for example, is generally understood to have represented a period of convergence around the issues of taxation, public spending and planning (see for example Deakin, 1988, pp. 24–8); while, as Hill (1993, p. 157) has argued, the universalist/selectivist debate cannot be totally explained on party political lines. Thus Labour breached the principle of universalism in its espousal of NHS charges in 1950, while it was during Margaret Thatcher's period as Secretary of State for Education in the early 1970s that the largest number of plans for comprehensive school reorganization were approved.

Differences within – as well as between – political parties are also a feature of this period. Within Conservatism the tension was between those who supported a tax-cutting and individual-initiative agenda, and those advocates of full employment and collectivism. The former was the basis of Assheton's opposition to the Beveridge proposals in the 1940s, the party's concern with regaining the middle-class vote, and Thorneycroft's resignation as Chancellor of the Exchequer in the 1950s and the re-shaping of Conservative policy in the second half of the 1960s. But it was not until after the failure of the Heath government in 1974 that the so-called 'New Right' began to win supporters on a large scale and to shape the rhetoric and ultimately the policies of the Thatcher governments after 1979. For much of the period covered in this chapter its influence lay beyond the day-to-day activities of the Party whether in government or opposition. In this respect, the agenda-setting of the Institute of Economic Affairs (IEA) founded in 1957 is of some importance. Through its publications programme the IEA sought

> to demonstrate the efficacy of economic liberalism and to apply the principles of the free market to all areas of economic activity from the telephone service to the welfare state, areas where the governing Butskellite consensus of the 'mixed' economy assumed that there was no alternative to the overwhelming state involvement of the day. (Cockett, 1995, p. 142)

Labour also had its divisions. Before the end of Attlee's premiership there were well-publicized differences between those led by Morrison who wanted 'consolidation' of the 1940s legislative programme, and those on the left of the party led by Bevan who sought advances towards socialism. Once the Left realized 'how far the party's historic agenda of nationalisation commitments and its new ability to reduce unemployment fell short of a social transformation, it rediscovered its distinctive voice' (Ceadel, 1991, p. 268). That 'distinctive voice' featured in many of the Labour Party debates of the 1950s: the introduction of NHS charges, the proposal to abolish clause 4 of the Labour Party Constitution, and in support of nuclear disarmament. There were, however, powerful countervailing arguments from those such as Anthony Crosland whose book *The Future of Socialism* (1956) has been described as 'one of the classics of post-war socialist revisionism' (Thompson, 1996, p. 151). For Crosland, Labour's traditional objective of public ownership was no longer of central importance. In the conditions of rising national prosperity, his policy agenda centred on economic growth which, he believed, would produce a fiscal dividend for government to invest in public services.

It was, ironically, the ex-Bevanite Harold Wilson who carried the revisionist agenda into his political programme after 1964. 'Wilson's achievement was to subordinate socialism to the proposition that Labour was better equipped than its rival to modernise the country's political institutions and to preside over economic growth' (Searle, 1995, p. 230). The failure of the economic growth strategy, however, provided the opportunity for the resurgence of the Labour left. Its increasing control of Labour's policy-making body – the National Executive – provided the opportunity to develop a more radical programme. According to Coates (1980, p. 2) 'the shift to the left in language and programme after 1970 was on a scale last seen as long ago as 1931'. But economic factors, including the oil-price rise of 1973 and parliamentary arithmetic enabled the parliamentary leadership to bypass the more radical proposals in the interests of projecting itself as a responsible party of government.

The Changing Statutory Sector

This section charts the principal changes in the statutory sector of welfare between 1951 and 1976 in terms of administrative organization, economic considerations and policy developments.

Administrative Organization

The restructuring of administrative arrangements and the creation of new, larger and more unified government departments reached its apogee in the decade between 1964 and 1974. As such, it can be seen to be representative of the managerialism and modernization which often underpinned the efforts of politicians at that time to solve Britain's economic and political problems (Dorey, 1996, p. 67). Examples included the fusion of the separate central government departments of Social Security and Health into the Department of Health and Social Security in 1968; the creation of generic, all-purpose local Social Services Departments in 1971, integrating the previously disparate responsibilities of Children's, Health and Welfare departments; and the implementation in 1974 of new arrangements for the administration of the NHS which had been the subject of protracted negotiation since 1967. This period also saw the publication of the Fulton Report on the Civil Service (1968) and in 1974 the first significant reorganization of local government since the end of the nineteenth century.

There were also earlier examples of organizational change. One of the earliest transferred responsibility for housing from the Ministry of Health to the newly-created Ministry of Housing and Local Government in 1951. Two years later, the Ministry of Pensions and National Insurance was created from two separate departments, but it was not until 1966 that a newly-created Ministry of Social Security became responsible for both insurance and means-tested benefits. At that time the National Assistance Board was replaced by the Supplementary Benefits Commission designed 'to act as an advisory body to the Ministry and as the body responsible for the discretionary elements in the means tested benefit system' (Hill, 1990, p. 44). This administrative change was coupled with reforms making individual entitlement to supplementary benefit more explicit. In 1968 the recently integrated Ministry of Social Security was amalgamated with the Ministry of Health to form the Department of Health and Social Security (DHSS). For Morgan (1990, p. 311) this suggested 'a new organisational direction for the welfare state, with a revival of the war-time ethic of comprehensiveness, planning and big government'. Others were less sanguine. Brown (1975, pp. 284–5), for example, raised the issue of functional coherence in circumstances where 'the two sides of the department have little in common and operate in more or less separate wings'.

At the same time as the administrative merger took place that created the DHSS, the first steps were taken towards the reorganization of the NHS. As Klein (1995, p. 82) notes, by the late 1960s there was general agreement that the structure created in 1948 'represented political expediency not administrative logic'. It was equally recognized by politicians that the preferred solution of a unification between health and local authority services was not feasible because of long-standing opposition from the medical profession. With that effectively ruled out, the aims of the reorganization were designed to achieve co-terminosity of boundaries between units of health administration and local authority services, and to improve the management system of the NHS itself. Each of these goals was achieved in the 1974 reorganization, though at the price of bureaucratic complexity and continuing division between hospitals and primary health care services.

Education, housing and personal welfare remained features of 'the local government welfare state' (Butcher, 1995, p. 37). In the case of the first two, central government responsibility changed – to the enlarged Department of Education and Science created in 1964, and from the Ministry of Housing and Local Government to the Department of the Environment created in 1970. But despite the recommendations in the Seebohm Report (1968) no action was taken to create a central government department concerned with personal welfare. Thus although the services were integrated at local level from 1971, responsibility in central government remained divided between the Home Office and the DHSS.

There is much discussion in the literature of the expansion of the local welfare state and of the partnership between central and local government that accompanied it. Relations between the partners were not always harmonious, however, and by the end of the period were becoming less so. The opposition of Labour councillors in Clay Cross, Derbyshire to the Conservative's Housing Finance Act of 1972 illustrates the conflict; while in matters of secondary school reorganization the Tameside case of 1976, involving local Conservative opposition to the Labour government's comprehensive programme, achieved a certain notoriety. Within the parameters of partnership the relationship was changing and dynamic, not least because of ideological politics – both of the Left and the Right – and increasing financial restraint.

Economic Considerations

Administrative and organizational change was one feature of a developing concern with modernization that to a degree united the political parties in government during the 1960s. In its broadest context it was part of the 'flirtation with planning' (Middleton, 1996a, p. 490) that accompanied the rush for growth in contradistinction to the 'stop–go' economic policies that had characterized the 1950s:

> In the 'Go' phase of the cycle, the domestic economy would expand, pushing down unemployment and pushing up spending. The increased spending would suck in imports, putting pressure on the balance of payments, and fuel inflation. This would prompt the government to bring in a package of tax increases and credit restrictions in order to choke off demand. The economy would then move into the 'Stop' phase of the cycle, whereby demand would fall, economic

growth would slow down and unemployment would rise. (Howlett, 1994, p. 328)

For Tomlinson (1996, p. 283) the Conservatives' economic policy of the 1950s was a 'lurching from expedient to expedient, in part at least because of the competing claims of liberty and order'. These different ideological presuppositions came under more sustained critique from the end of the 1950s as Britain's economic position *vis-à-vis* that of competitor countries received increased attention. That, in turn, it has been suggested, shifted the direction of political action in favour of indicative planning on the French model, and an increasingly corporatist approach to economic affairs brought the Conservatives 'nearer to embracing a corporatist state and dirigiste society than ever before or since' (Dutton, 1997, p. 73). Meanwhile, under the Labour leader Harold Wilson 'planning was elevated to almost celebrity status' (Middleton, 1996a, p. 494) with planning expanded to include prices and incomes as well as regional policies.

Economic growth through planning not only held out the prospect of improving Britain's economic performance. It also offered the possibility of improving domestic living standards and the amount spent on social welfare programmes while protecting worker's take-home pay. Governments thus became responsible not only for creating the framework of growth but also for ensuring the distribution of its fruits. In 1959 the Conservative election manifesto stated as its objective 'to double the standard of living in this generation and to ensure that all sections of society share in the expansion of wealth' (Craig, 1975, p. 215). Labour's counterpart in the 1964 election asserted that as 'economic expansion increases our national wealth we shall see to it that the needs of the community are increasingly met' (*ibid.*, p. 263). This entailed better education, decent housing, a modernized health service, and improved financial provision for old people and widows.

In this way, for both parties in government 'the politics of the 1960s was social politics' (Glennerster, 1995a, p. 96). In welfare, the mood was one of planning and expansion, a combination that continued until 1976. Social expenditure which had risen by 4.2 per cent between 1951 and 1964, increased by 5.9 per cent in the Wilson governments of 1964 to 1970, and by an annual average of 6.8 per cent during the Heath government of 1970 to 1974 (Lowe, 1996a, p. 191). It did so against a background of the recurrent balance-of-payments crises and the devaluation of sterling of the Wilson governments and the longer-term failure of Labour and Conservative administrations to arrest Britain's relative economic decline. That became part of the economic crisis of the welfare state, whose impact will be discussed in the final section of this chapter.

Policy Development

This section looks first at two of the services of the local welfare state – housing and education – before reviewing changes in social security.

As we noted in the last chapter, the main direction of postwar housing policy was making good the effects of war damage and destruction. That policy continued until the mid-1950s, by which time 'the housing shortage was considered to have been all but resolved' (Lowe, 1993, p. 247). By contrast with the emphasis on council-house building of the Labour programme, Conservative policy tended to be more flexible. In 1951 only 25 000 houses were built by the private sector compared to 171 000 built for the local authorities. The Conservative's lifting of restrictions on land use and the abolition of building licenses in 1954 significantly altered the balance. In 1956 private house building had increased to 126 000 houses, while local authority housing showed only a small (but continuing) increase to 181 000. It was in fact during the years 1952 to 1956 that the largest number of council houses to be built in a four-year period was achieved under a Conservative government. Not surprisingly, Macmillan as the Minister of Housing 'was seen as one of the government's stars' and his success undoubtedly helped to propel him to the premiership (Ramsden, 1995, p. 257).

There was in this period a continuing change in housing tenure. Owner-occupation and local authority rental increased while private rental declined. This is usually attributed to the existence of subsidies for the former – whether in the form of mortgage-interest tax relief or construction subsidies. No such subsidies were available for the private rented sector; and despite the stimulus which the Conservatives offered by the abolition of rent controls in 1957, it proved inadequate. Labour's introduction of fair rents and greater protection for sitting tenants further reduced the financial benefits to landlords, and where house prices were rising the sale of properties became more attractive than rental. Meanwhile, as the financial advantages associated with home ownership increased, so those who could afford to buy did so. Often they were the newly-affluent, two-earner families for whom housing increasingly represented a sense of security and an economic investment.

The doubling of those in owner-occupation between 1945 and 1976 also had its impact on local authority housing. It was those households with lower incomes, out of employment and less able to obtain mortgages who were increasingly concentrated in this sector. Council housing which had ended the 1940s as 'the most modern and best equipped and therefore attractive to affluent households, ended the 1970s with an image tarnished by an ageing stock and problems of design, maintenance, repair and management' (Murie, 1995, p. 131).

Education had a high political profile throughout the period between 1951 and 1976. Initially it featured as a target for cuts in public spending. Ironically, the Chancellor who sought them was the same R. A. Butler who, as President of the Board of Education, had been responsible for the 1944 Education Act. From the mid-1950s, however, the twin themes of expansion and equality dominated the policy agenda.

David Eccles, who saw it as his mission to bring to education something of the 'feeling of expansion and success which has been the mark of the housing drive' (Simon, 1991, p. 111), was much associated with expansion. New school buildings were constructed, the number of teachers in training increased and a wide range of official inquiries was begun into all aspects of education. Education was increasingly linked to Britain's economic and commercial competitiveness and a growing share of public resources was devoted to it. In the light of the emphasis placed by politicians of the time on science and technology, however, it is paradoxical that the secondary technical schools virtually ceased to exist and became absorbed into the comprehensive schools of the 1960s (Sanderson, 1991, pp. 159–82).

From the late 1950s the issue that dominated educational debate and policy-making was that of equality and, in particular, the replacement of selective secondary education by comprehensive schools. By the beginning of the 1960s a considerable body of research evidence had called into question the tripartite inheritance of the 1944 Education Act. Educational selection at 11+ appeared to be 'to a disconcerting degree a process of social selection disguised as academic selection' (Wooldridge, 1996, p. 244), while psychological research had called into question the objective nature of the testing and blown a serious hole in the notion that there was a fixed pool of ability limiting the numbers of those who were thought capable of benefiting from a grammar school education. Such evidence increasingly won the political support of those who accepted that there was considerable under-developed talent among schoolchildren which could be harnessed more effectively to the benefit of economic growth as well as individual improvement. This view received official endorsement in the Crowther (1959) and Newsom (1963) Reports.

It was not surprising, then, that within a year of Labour being returned to power in 1964, Anthony Crosland introduced his Circular 10/65 requesting – but not requiring – local authorities to submit plans for the reorganization of secondary education which would end selection at 11+. The following year government cash for new school buildings became conditional on local authorities agreeing to go comprehensive.

Given Labour's commitment to multilateral or comprehensive schools almost from the time it left office in 1951, Crosland's decision of 1965 was hardly surprising. It is important, therefore, to recognize that he was confirming and extending the practice of a growing number of local authorities. By 1963, it has been estimated, 90 of the 163 local education authorities in England and Wales were in the process of reorganizing their secondary schooling. Pressure from the local authorities themselves had rendered inadequate the Eccles criteria for the development of comprehensive schools. These were that they should only be initiated in rural areas with sparse populations or on new housing estates where there were no existing schools. Those criteria were officially laid to rest by Edward Boyle, Eccles' successor at the Ministry of Education. It was a signal to local authorities that their reorganization plans had some chance of success, even if they involved grammar schools which the Conservatives had hitherto been committed to defending. And it remains one of the quirks of educational policy that the largest number of comprehensive schools were approved in the early 1970s during Mrs Thatcher's period as Secretary of State for Education.

By that time the opposition to comprehensivization was already beginning with the publication after 1968 of the so-called Black papers. These publications gave shape in the 1970s to a developing critique of progressive education and child-centred pedagogies. Their rhetoric became part of the 'the great debate' on education launched in 1976 by the Labour Prime Minister, James Callaghan. 'Education had become too concerned with giving children a good time, standards were too low and schooling was too little geared to the needs of a modern economy' (Glennerster, 1995a, p. 169). This was the agenda that the Conservatives would develop during the 1980s when the issue of equality was displaced politically by the discourse of freedom and choice.

In the sphere of income maintenance the paradox of this period was 'the rediscovery of poverty' in the midst of 'the affluent society'. The period began with a sense of complacency. The third of Rowntree's investigations of York published in 1951 expressed the dominant theme of the 1950s. The combination of full employment and the welfare state had produced the situation in which poverty – certainly in the prewar understanding of the term – had been abolished. It was no longer poverty, but prosperity and affluence that were the principal features of the postwar world. The new phenomenon was that of 'the affluent worker' (Goldthorpe, 1969) increasingly able to afford the increasing range of consumer goods that were available.

This complacency was shattered by the output of academic studies during the 1960s which cumulatively challenged the egalitarianism of the welfare state. Such studies not only redefined poverty as relative deprivation (Townsend and Abel-Smith, 1965), their research findings also revealed that despite the spread of affluence and the establishment of the welfare state, poverty persisted among clearly defined sections of the population. These included large families on low incomes and those among the retired and unemployed who failed to take up the means-tested National Assistance benefits for which they were eligible. The academic research of the time thus constituted a critique both of the principles and the practical operation of the social security system.

That system itself was changing. In 1959 the Conservative government effectively abandoned the Beveridge model by the introduction of the earnings-related pension scheme, a technique that was subsequently applied to other insurance benefits in 1975. Already in 1957 the Conservatives had capped the level of contributions to the National Insurance Fund as part of its concern with rising levels of public expenditure. Graduated contributions thus represented an alternative form of revenue-raising; but there were other advantages to the scheme. As Lowe (1993, p. 143) notes, 'by providing an earnings-related supplement to the flat-rate pension it had the potential to lift many older people off means-tested benefits and to provide some reward for hard work'. Labour, too, had abandoned its commitment to the flat-rate principle in a policy document published in 1957. By the end of the 1950s, therefore, there was 'the start of a cross-party consensus on pensions that broke radically with Beveridge' (Sullivan, 1996, p. 226). Subsequent governments – both Labour and Conservative – built upon the earnings-related pension in proposals developed during the 1960s and 1970s, though with differences of emphasis.

Labour's 1969 scheme, for example, emphasized state provision and a redistributive formula that favoured lower-paid workers. By contrast, the Conservative proposals in 1973 outlined a residual role for the state pension as part of a strategy designed to encourage growth in occupational pension schemes. Given their different objectives, it is interesting that Labour's further attempt at pensions reform in 1975 – the introduction of the State Earnings Related Pension Scheme (SERPS) – received all-party support. That, it has been suggested, may have been the result of the compromises embodied in the Act (Deacon, 1995, p. 84). Its central provisions allowed individuals to opt out of the state scheme if they were already in private schemes judged adequate by the government; provided an enhanced state pension scheme for all other working people; and 'embodied a new presumption that women were normally economically independent individuals, though there might be phases of the life-cycle when they were engaged on 'other duties' (Joshi and Davies, 1994, p. 236). At the time, this made the scheme 'the most advanced in the world in terms of equal rights for women and carers' (Glennerster, 1995a, p. 114).

There was less concern until the late 1960s about the issue of child and family poverty. The period was marked by a continuing commitment to the universalism of family allowances. But in real terms their value declined considerably. Until their up-rating in 1968, family allowances had remained at the level set in 1952. Over that period their real value had fallen by one-third. The academic research of the 1960s highlighted *inter alia* the poverty of the low-waged working poor, and it was one of the concerns of the Child Poverty Action Group (CPAG) established in 1965. Finlayson (1994, p. 340) comments caustically that 'the branches of the CPAG were co-incident less with poor families than with the existence of universities': a reference to both the academic inquiries in which CPAG engaged as well as to the middle-class welfare professionals who predominated among its membership. To its policy of highlighting inadequate benefits has been attributed a doubling of the level of family allowances introduced in 1968, though it was paid for by a 'claw back' from child tax allowances.

A further change came with the replacement of family allowances by child benefit in 1976. Unlike family allowances, child benefit was paid also in respect of first children and was not taxable. The simultaneous withdrawal of child tax allowances potentially represented a transfer of resources from the man's wage packet to the mother's purse. Fearful of the reaction of male trade union members in the midst of the Labour government's pay restraint, the child benefit programme was accordingly introduced in stages (McCarthy, 1986).

The alternative to up-rating and extending universal benefits was to target resources where they were most needed. This was the strategy adopted by the Conservative government with the introduction of Family Income Supplement (FIS) in 1971. Though it contradicted assurances given by the Conservatives to CPAG before the 1970 general election, under FIS working heads of families whose income was below a set scale would have half the difference made up in the form of a benefit for a six-month period. As such, 'it was the first direct subsidy of full time earnings since the 1834 Poor Law had brought the Speenhamland system to an end' (Vincent, 1991, p. 166). In practice, FIS ran into problems of low take-up and heightened the problems of the poverty trap. 'The subsidisation of low wages was compounding the tendency of means-tested relief to imprison the poor at or below subsistence level, penalising every increase in earnings by a corresponding loss of benefits' (*ibid.*, p. 167). As Lowe (1996a, p. 201) comments, 'this was no way to encourage the low paid to work harder'.

The example of FIS illustrates the growing complexity of the income maintenance system. Part of the explanation lay with the addition of new benefits such as those for disabled people and their carers introduced in the early 1970s as well as changes introduced at the same time to housing benefit. In addition, there was increasing awareness of the interaction of the tax and benefit systems and between benefit levels and work incentives. Both Labour in the 1960s and Conservatives in the early 1970s flirted with integrating the tax and benefit systems by means of income guarantees or social credit. Meanwhile, in 1973 Keith Joseph's separation of long from short-term benefits marked a shift away from the flat-rate principle. Underpinning these issues, however, was the developing discourse around eligibility and entitlement.

These themes were already part of the welfare rights movement agenda of the 1960s and 1970s in relation to the continuing and expanding role of means-tested benefits. In practice, welfare rights organizations initiated campaigns to improve take-up and assisted claimants in appealing decisions. In policy terms, however, opinion was divided between those who wished to see a strengthening of National Insurance benefits by means of regular up-rating and the introduction of earnings-related supplements, and those who advocated a more explicit entitlement to benefits in the National Assistance scheme which was renamed Supplementary Benefit (SB) in 1966. The creation of the unified Ministry of

Social Security at that time was designed to better integrate insurance and assistance benefits. But in practice, 'SB was still sharply distinguished from national insurance by the amount of discretion retained by local officers and particularly by their power to award additional weekly payments or lump sum grants to meet extra needs' (Deacon, 1995, p. 85). As the number of such discretionary payments continued to increase during the 1970s (Deacon and Bradshaw, 1983, p. 110), those responsible for managing its operation spoke of 'poor morale among staff. . . the misuse of discretion, and the danger of a general breakdown of the system' (Donnison, 1982, p. 215). It was primarily in response to this pressure that an internal review of SB was begun in 1976, though the changes proposed were not implemented until 1980.

The Moving Frontier

The period of the classic welfare state had consequences – not all of them predictable – for the other suppliers of welfare. This section examines in turn the voluntary sector and the provision of private, commercial welfare.

The popular stereotype is that the expansion of the statutory services of the welfare state 'crowded out' the activities of the voluntary sector, and that until the resurgence of voluntary activity in the mid-1960s the sector was simply 'marking time' (Wolfendon, 1978) or even 'moribund' (Knight, 1993).

That interpretation has recently been called into question. Finlayson (1994, pp. 288–93), for example, has drawn attention to the continuing role for the voluntary sector expressed in a variety of official reports of the period: Nathan in the early 1950s, Younghusband in the late 1950s and Seebohm in the late 1960s. Furthermore, the extent of practical work especially in personal welfare confirms the continuing importance of the sector. Data produced in the mid-1950s for the Younghusband Report, for example, indicated 'a considerable residue of voluntary agency activity utilised and part financed by local authorities' (Brenton, 1985, p. 27). In addition, voluntary activity was moving into new areas. These included medical research, environmental organizations and specialist support for disabled people.

There is little doubt, however, that this activity was taking place in an environment that had been changed by the social legislation of the 1940s.

'The general public . . . assumed that the new welfare legislation rendered charities redundant or obsolete, and no longer felt obliged to support them' (Finlayson, 1994, p. 298). The issue was not only that of financial volatility. There was also uncertainty about future direction, arising from the changing relationship between the state and the voluntary sector. As Margaret Simey (1951, p. 30) commented, 'the voluntary society and the voluntary worker feel that they are being constantly forced to shift their ground, though often unable to decide where to shift to'.

The creation of a whole cadre of new campaigning groups from the mid-1960s transformed the nature of the voluntary sector. Among the best known are the Child Poverty Action Group, the Disablement Income Group, Gingerbread and Shelter. Often inspired by the civil rights and feminist movements of the USA, these predominantly middle-class campaigners represented 'the beginning of a new wave of voluntary activity that was both complementary to and critical of the welfare state' (Taylor, 1995, p. 217). In addition, they provided a legitimacy for voluntary activity among many on the left of the political spectrum.

That changing environment occurred in parallel to the expansion of state sponsorship of voluntary action that began in the late 1960s. Initiatives such as the national Community Development Programme and Education Priority Area action research projects were characteristic of this changing approach. Much influenced by American initiatives such as the War on Poverty and Operation Headstart, they sought to provide 'state support for community based voluntary organisations seeking to develop neighbourhood-based activities involving local poor people' (Alcock, 1996, p. 91). As such they were a counterweight to the 'top-down' nature of the statutory welfare state and, at least in theory, provided an opportunity to develop increased citizen participation, which was one of the recurring themes in official reports of the period (Skeffington, 1969; Richardson, 1983).

Increasing involvement in state-initiated schemes and a growing reliance on state funding, however, raised the issue of the independence of the voluntary sector: an issue that became more pertinent as the voluntary sector became more associated with government programmes for the unemployed during the 1970s (Taylor, 1995, p. 228). Organizationally, this closer relationship between the statutory and voluntary sectors was confirmed by the establishment of the Voluntary Services Unit in the Home Office in 1972 which was designed to coordinate government policy towards the voluntary sector as a whole.

The period covered by this chapter ends with the publication of the Wolfendon Report. Anchored within a perspective of welfare pluralism, it was critical of the statutory welfare services: they were expensive, overly bureaucratic and epitomized the weaknesses of monopoly provision. In the Committee's view, there was a place both for voluntary organizations and for the sector, not least in humanizing the face of welfare and providing the opportunity for 'people . . . to join with others in devising means to meet their own needs or those of others they wish to help' (1978, p. 29). It was remarkably similar to Beveridge's apologia for voluntary action published exactly 30 years before.

The welfare state may have universalized welfare but it did not abolish the commercial sector. Private education and pay beds in the NHS hospitals were part of the settlement of the 1940s, while in the period of 'the fully fledged welfare state . . . private welfare continued to flourish and to jostle state provision' (Papadakis and Taylor-Gooby, 1987, p. 7). Labour in government vacillated on private education in the 1960s, while in the 1970s the threat of industrial action in the NHS forced it to broker a compromise on private provision. In housing, financial changes especially gave an impetus to the private market and owner occupation. On the one hand, the Conservatives de-controlled the advantageous interest rates to local authorities for house-building, and in 1956 allowed them to rise to a market level. On the other, a combination of factors coalesced to make mortgage-interest tax relief a more attractive proposition and hence to stimulate the move towards owner occupation. Tax relief on mortgage interest had been introduced in 1921, but its impact was limited until the 1950s. Thereafter, 'with tax thresholds dropping and house prices rising, the number of beneficiaries and the value of their hidden subsidy began to escalate' (Lowe, 1993, p. 255).

In addition to mortgage-interest tax relief, improvement grants provided a further benefit to owner occupiers. Reflecting the new emphasis on older parts of the housing stock, Labour's 1969 Housing Act introduced more generous housing improvement grants, with an immediate impact on the take-up, the figures increasing from 110 000 to over 350 000 between 1968 and 1974. Housing improvement grants constituted another manifestation of the growing cross-party commitment from the early 1960s towards owner-occupation, a trend that was especially significant for Labour given its preference for the public sector in the immediate postwar period.

Pension arrangements were characterized by a 'complex inter-meshing of state and private initiatives' (Papadakis and Taylor-Gooby, 1987,

p. 103). This was the result both of the historical inheritance and of changes which were introduced during this period. Occupational pension schemes for male civil servants and in parts of the public sector already had a considerable history when the state pension scheme began. And during the interwar period there was a considerable expansion of company group and provident schemes. During the quarter century covered by this chapter, such occupational and private pension arrangements 'proceeded in great strength' (Finlayson, 1994, p. 295), though even towards the end of the period there were significant discrepancies in coverage. Men were more likely to be covered than women and non-manual workers predominated (CSO, *Social Trends*, 1972),

Tax relief was again one factor in the continuing spread of occupational and private schemes. By 1956–57 the cost to the Treasury of such relief had reached £120 million a year (Hannah, 1986, p. 45). Another was the 'contracting-out' of the graduated element in the state scheme which was introduced in the 1959 National Insurance Act. 'The insurance companies stepped up their selling efforts, finding a ready response among employers who were now bound to contribute to the state graduated scheme' (*ibid.*, p. 59). Between 1956 and 1967, for example, the total number of employees with occupational pensions increased from 4.3 million to 12.2 million (Walker, 1986, p. 202). The subsequent decline in occupational pension coverage in the private sector led the Conservative government to introduce tax concessions in 1970 and 1971. A further challenge for private and occupational pensions, however, was Labour's 1975 pensions reform offering generous benefits, inflation-proofing and an improved deal for women. In the event, Labour used the state scheme as a model for private and occupational schemes and, as part of the politics of pensions, offered subsidies to commercial suppliers as the means of ensuring Conservative Party support for other features of the pensions package.

Both the voluntary sector and the private market operated in changed conditions in the period of the classic welfare state. Yet they remained part of the mixed economy of welfare and many of their activities were underpinned by state funding. Here the similarities end: for whereas especially from the 1960s the voluntary sector became increasingly radicalized and diversified its activities, the commercial sector retained many of the hallmarks that had characterized it earlier in the century.

Crisis

In the 1970s the social policy literature became increasingly doom-laden and eschatological. The British welfare state was – to use a word much in vogue at the time – in crisis. In its characteristic depiction that crisis was a compound of three factors: economic, political and social.

As the phenomenon of economic growth came to an end, Britain in the 1970s appeared locked into an intractable combination of rising unemployment and escalating inflation, low productivity, declining industrial investment and profitability and heightened industrial conflict. Such a combination had obvious implications for the maintenance – let alone the expansion – of the public sector of welfare. To those factors, however, was added the oil price rise imposed by the oil-producing countries in 1973, which had the effect of enormously increasing Britain's public-sector borrowing requirement. A public spending 'squeeze' was introduced in order to restore the confidence of the market and cash limits on spending departments intensified the pressure on public programmes. Further measures became necessary in 1976 as a precipitous fall in sterling occurred. The terms of the loan negotiated with the International Monetary Fund necessitated a further cut of £1 billion from public spending in 1977–78, with a similar amount being raised by a National Insurance surcharge on employers.

The consequences of such measures in higher unemployment and the reduction in welfare programmes were regarded as an anathema by the resurgent Labour left for whom the social and economic objectives of the 1940s settlement were 'the touchstone of socialism' (Shaw, 1996, p. 182). It was, however, the Labour Prime Minister James Callaghan who sounded the death knell of Keynesianism in his speech to the 1976 Labour Party conference:

> We used to think that you could just spend your way out of recession and increase employment by cutting taxes and boosting government spending...that option no longer exists. (cited in Dutton, 1997, p. 108)

The economic crisis was 'a watershed for the government...[which] finally drew a line under Keynesian policies and the idea that the conquest of unemployment was government's first responsibility' (Thorpe, 1997, p. 194). Between 1976 and 1979 unemployment averaged over 5 per cent, double what it had been in the 1950s and 1960s, with a consequent impact on social security benefits and the loss of tax revenue. But perhaps most importantly of all, Callaghan's speech legitimated the anti-Keynesian, monetarist critique of Margaret Thatcher who had been elected Conservative Party leader in 1975. In that sense, Thatcherism pre-dates Thatcher's period as Prime Minister.

There is a strong interrelationship between the economic and political dimensions of the welfare state 'crisis'. The Bacon–Eltis thesis of the mid-1970s, for example, contended that ever-increasing public welfare expenditure had deflected resources away from manufacturing industry and thereby contributed to the deterioration of Britain's economic performance (Bacon and Eltis, 1978, p. 16).

There were a number of variations on this theme. Some highlighted the increasingly powerful role of public-sector trade unions; others, the growing difficulties for government macro-economic management in an increasingly global economy. The consequence was a crisis of ungovernability, of government overload and loss of legitimacy. 'Governments have tried to play God. They have failed. But they go on trying. How can they be made to stop?' (King, 1975, p. 296). The apparent solution was 'a return to sanity – to economic and social *laissez-faire*, to voluntarism and the minimal state' (Mishra, 1984, p. 42): the elements, in short, of the neo-Conservative agenda that was to be offered as an ideological alternative by the resurgent Conservative Party with Margaret Thatcher as its new leader.

Paradoxically, that neo-conservative agenda was aided by the critique of the welfare state that had been developed by the political Left in the late 1960s and early 1970s. Successive studies showed the welfare state to be falling short of egalitarian expectations: poverty persisted, the middle classes had disproportionately benefited from the availability of universal services, and meanwhile unemployment was on an upward curve. Marxist writers at the same time argued that notions of crisis and contradiction were implicit in the welfare state. Rather than representing an improvement for the working class, the welfare state had served to make capitalism more efficient and productive and, as an agent of social control, had been a means of maintaining the *status quo* of class relations (Gough, 1979). Ideologically, therefore, the welfare state was under attack from Left and Right.

Interwoven with the economic and political manifestations of 'crisis' was a third dimension: the loss of popular legitimacy. Two factors are of especial importance in this regard: the increasing tax burden on individuals and the media- highlighted phenomenon of 'scrounger-phobia'.

The inflation of the 1970s brought more workers within the income tax net which generated increasing resentment. In the same decade there was a growing awareness of – and antipathy to – public expenditure:

> In the 'good times' when people's earnings are rising, they may be willing to afford altruistic policies... supporting a benefit which will largely go to others. But times of 'economic stress' such as the 1970s tend to be associated with 'less generosity' and a preference for 'spending cuts over taxation'. (Alt, 1979, p. 259)

That applied especially to the social security agenda, where the media headlines about 'scroungers' reinforced anti-altruistic feelings. Golding and Middleton's (1982) study of press and public attitudes at the time indicated the shift away from cases of individual abuse to journalistic reporting which called into question the wider operation of the social security system itself. This became the basis of a popular welfare backlash recounting the alleged experiences of social security claimants living a life of luxury 'on the dole' financed by increasing taxes on those in work. It was a powerful association of ideas and experiences, and it undoubtedly contributed to the popularity of the Conservatives' 1979 election manifesto with its pledge to cut taxes, reduce the bureaucracy of government and emphasise greater personal responsibility. How such values shaped the Thatcherite welfare state is the subject of the next chapter.

4

REAPPRAISAL

> Margaret Thatcher... honestly believed that she was leading a crusade for national regeneration. And in the holy war which was to make Britain strong and free, there was no time to weep for the inevitable casualties.
>
> (Hattersley, 1997, p. 268)

Just before Margaret Thatcher became Prime Minister in 1979 with a majority of 43 seats in the House of Commons, James Callaghan, the out-going Labour Prime Minister, observed a 'sea-change in politics' of the kind which happened every thirty years or so in British public life and which it was beyond the capacity of any politician to alter or control (Donoughue, 1987, p. 191). Some of the dimensions of that 'sea change' have been analysed in the previous chapter. It was an image which Conservatives associated with the Thatcherite project liked to emphasize. One of them – Nigel Lawson – expressed it thus: 'Our chosen course does represent a distinct and self-conscious break from the predominantly social democratic assumptions that have hitherto underlain policy in post-war Britain' (cited Kavanagh, 1987, p. 13).

Even among those who argue that the governments of the 1980s represented a radical break with the past, opinions differ about their impact on the classic welfare state. For some, the politics of the period represented its destruction at the hands of expenditure cuts, the disengagement of the state from welfarism and its progressive privatization. For others, who focus on the survival of the institutions of the welfare state, it is restructuring that is the major legacy of the 1980s. Quasi-markets, competition and consumer choice, the introduction of businesslike notions of efficiency and effectiveness symbolized the creation of a new management of welfare. On this analysis 'the institutions were reformed rather than abolished' (Flynn, 1997, p. 36).

Thatcher and Thatcherism

A considerable literature exists on Thatcherism and the government of the 1980s, and a number of themes recur which are relevant to the present discussion.

First, Thatcherism was both a personality cult – focussed upon a strong leader who epitomized conviction politics – and an ideology which contained at its heart the paradox of 'the free economy and the strong state'. It thus held in tension 'a liberal tendency which argues the case for a freer, more open and more competitive economy, and a conservative tendency which is more interested in restoring social and political authority throughout society' (Gamble, 1988, pp. 28–9). Both of these strands in Thatcherism were critical of the welfare state. Free-market liberals saw it as a disincentive to investment and as 'stifling the potential vibrancy of a free market economy', while neo-conservatives were especially critical of its dependency culture and favoured 'a centrally imposed moral authoritarianism enforcing a return to "traditional" values' and 'the active intervention of the state to police and coerce deviant miscreants' (Hay, 1996, pp. 134–5). Thatcherism's electoral appeal lay in its blending of the divergent promises of freedom and order, choice and discipline appealing both to 'new aspirations, and ... old values' (Marquand, 1988b, p. 171).

Secondly, there is the issue of periodization. So far the Thatcherite project has been presented as a uniform activity stretching from the time of her election as leader of the Conservative Party in 1975 to the end of her Prime Ministerial career in 1990. Most analyses (for example, Jessop, 1988), however, suggest that its nature changed over time and that it should be examined in terms of periodization. In this account, Thatcherism began as a social movement borne out of economic decline, government overload and middle-class resentment. This was the 'authoritarian populism' of Thatcherism:

Thatcherism's success…does not lie in its capacity to dupe unsus-
pecting folk, but in the way it addresses real problems, real and lived
experiences, real contradictions – yet it is able to represent them
within a logic of discourse which pulls them systematically into line
with policies and class strategies of the right. (Hall, 1979, p. 39)

It was such a logic of discourse that created the conditions for electoral
success in 1979. Thereafter, the Thatcherite project acquired different
facets in subsequent periods: control over party, government and
Cabinet which was largely achieved by 1982; the curbing of trade
union power and the symbolic defeat of the miners, the introduction
of the privatization programme, and some changes in social welfare
especially in social security up to the mid-1980s. The third phase
began with the Conservatives' third successive election victory in 1987
and represents what Hay termed (1996, p. 148) 'radical Thatcherism'.
It incorporates much of the change that was introduced into the
welfare state as well as the celebrated debacle of the poll tax which
ultimately contributed to Mrs Thatcher's downfall in 1990. For Morgan
(1990, p. 489) the years between 1987 and 1990 were the 'high noon' of
Thatcherism in which 'the new radicalism now showed itself in full.
The legacy of the Second World War and the Attlee government, the
very notion of the mixed economy as familiarised by "Butskellism" was
being dismantled'.
    This raises the third issue, which concerns the origins of Thatcherism.
The evidence portrays it as a diverse inheritance. Margaret Thatcher
herself acknowledged the influence of being brought up in a lower-
middle-class home in Grantham in the years between the wars, where
the influence of her father – a largely self-educated local grocer, Alder-
man and Methodist local preacher – was especially significant. 'The
political life with its parallel attractions of service and of power was the
only life set before her as a model superior to that of shop- keeping'
(Young, 1990, p. 3).
    There was, however, more to Thatcherism than the personal experi-
ences of childhood and adolescence. In its formative period in the years
of high inflation in the mid-1970s, intellectual ballast was provided by
two Nobel prize-winning economists – Hayek and Friedman:

Friedman taught that inflation could be reduced only by restricting
the money supply, while Hayek argued for the supremacy of the
free market, in which individuals would be free to pursue their

choices within a framework regulated by price and law. (Seldon, 1994, p. 58)

Common to both was a rejection of Keynesian orthodoxy, though they differed in the application of monetarism as a practical policy (Gamble, 1988, p. 44).

Whatever the differences between Hayek and Friedman, it was the conversion of Keith Joseph, who like Margaret Thatcher had been a minister in Edward Heath's government, to their ideas that proved decisive in the shaping of Thatcherism. A crucial development was the establishment of the Centre for Policy Studies as a research institute and pressure group. Joseph was its Chairman, Margaret Thatcher a director and Alfred Sherman its Director of Studies. Its aim in the long term was to change 'the whole climate of liberal-left, anti-enterprise popular opinion' (Dutton, 1997, p. 116). Thatcher's election as party leader in 1975 made the attainment of that objective more feasible; though there were many among her own MPs who did not support her crusade.

When implemented as a practical policy, monetarism signalled the abandonment of any political commitment to 'maintain a high and stable level of employment'. As we have already noted in the previous chapter, however, its implicit abandonment had been pre-figured by Callaghan in 1976. In its place, the conquest of inflation was firmly established as an overriding objective of the Thatcher-led Conservative government when it returned to power in 1979. Initially this was pursued by the Friedmanite prescription of reducing the money supply (the measure known as M3) and then, after the formal abandonment of monetary targets from the mid-1980s, by means of interest-rate rises and the parity of sterling. The rate of inflation which had been 10 per cent in 1979 and 20 per cent in 1981 fell to 4 per cent by 1983. Over the same period, however, unemployment rose to over 3 million and during the 1980s as a whole it never returned to its pre-1979 level. Its unprecedentedly high postwar level conjured up images of the 1930s. As then, unemployment highlighted certain persisting social divisions and 'an increasing segregation of experience between North and South, between smoke stack and sunrise industries, and between redundant employees with little prospect of new jobs and people in work with rising incomes' (Clarke, 1992, pp. 304–5). The talk was once again of a divided Britain; and one of the paradoxes for political scientists is how, despite such conditions and experiences, the Conservatives led by Margaret Thatcher won three successive election victories.

Part of the answer lies in the factionalism and weakness that characterized the Labour Party for much of the 1980s. This factionalism was both of the Left and the Right: the latter symbolized by the creation of the Social Democratic Party in 1981, the former by the well-publicised activities of Militant Tendency, a Trotskyite organization which sought to radicalize Labour from within. Electorally, Labour's fortunes slumped. In the 1983 general election Labour's share of the vote was its lowest since 1918, and with only 209 seats its worst parliamentary performance since 1935. At that election Labour attracted the support of only 38 per cent of skilled workers, while its share of the non-manual vote was the lowest since the Second World War. Dorey (1995, p. 165) argues that the support of the skilled working class was especially significant to the Conservative's political fortunes throughout the 1980s. Thatcherism, he suggests, appealed to both their material and moral instincts. Tax cuts, share ownership and council-house sales offered them material advantages, while the 'strong state' elements of Thatcherite Conservatism reinforced 'the deeply rooted prejudice with which the working class has long been afflicted – its xenophobia and racism, its "lock 'em up" attitude towards law breakers and its virulent anti-intellectualism'.

Within the new political milieu staked out by Thatcherism, Labour shifted its stance considerably (Ellison, 1997, p. 51). 'Its 1989 policy review amounted to a wholesale abandonment of its 1983 and 1987 programmes and was the least socialist policy statement published in the history of the party' (Crewe, 1996, p. 405). It dropped the wealth tax proposal, abandoned any commitment to return to penal levels of taxation and refused to restore trade unions' former legal immunities. In addition, 'it adopted Thatcher's language of markets and individualism ... In effect the Labour Party jettisoned socialism in all but name and turned itself into a party of private enterprise and the free market' (ibid., pp. 405–6). Labour too became part of 'the great moving right show' (Hall, 1979).

If nationally the Labour Party was unable to either offer an alternative or an effective opposition to Thatcherism, there were other centres where resistance was located. Chief among them were local government, the trade unions and public sector professions. During the Thatcher hegemony each of them was progressively emasculated.

Labour had established a strong base in local government which thus constituted an alternative power base around which opposition forces could muster. The Greater London Council (GLC) along with Liverpool and Lambeth were the manifest leaders of such opposition, but there were many more pilloried by the Conservatives as 'loony left' councils which, so they argued, were being profligate with public funds especially favouring the interests of minority groups. The Conservative response to these alternative power bases was three-fold. First, the GLC and the metropolitan county councils, which had only been established in 1974, were abolished. Secondly, rate capping was introduced, which allowed a central government minister to set a ceiling on the amount which local authorities could raise via the system of local taxation or rates. Thirdly, some of the functions of local authorities were removed. The sale of council houses introduced in 1980 was one example of this process, but it subsequently included 'opt outs' for schools introduced in the 1988 Education Act and the requirement of compulsory competitive tendering which introduced the principles of market discipline into the supply of local government services. These changes represented an attack on the principle of local authority autonomy and on the notion of 'partnership' between central and local government that was perceived as one of the essential ingredients of the postwar consensus.

Another element of that consensus was the incorporation of the trade unions from the 1960s into the economic planning process through their membership of the National Economic Development Council. Coincidentally, it is from exactly that period that trade unions came to be perceived as a cause of Britain's declining economic performance. That perception was built around the links between wage levels and inflation, restrictive practices in industry and the issue of strike action. When Margaret Thatcher became Prime Minister in 1979, trade union membership was at an all-time peak of 13.5 million. By 1991 it stood at 9.5 million, by which time union density at just over 34 per cent was at its lowest since the 1940s (Thorpe, 1997, p. 215).

During the 1980s, three changes are particularly significant. First, trade union representation on a wide variety of commissions and advisory bodies was greatly reduced and the institutions of corporatist planning were either abolished or met less frequently and exerted less influence. Secondly, legislative measures were introduced which removed the legal immunity of trade unions holding a strike without a ballot, required regular voting on the retention of political funds and empowered secret ballots. This created a new *modus operandi* for the trade union movement. Thirdly, there was the well-publicized political attempt to democratize the movement, wresting power away from its leaders and vesting it with 'ordinary' trade union members themselves. It was an appeal to 'decent, hard working, politically moderate, patriotic people who were all too often manipulated and misled by their allegedly extremist, politically motivated, power hungry union leaders' (Dorey, 1995, p. 176).

Like the trade unions, professional associations had been a source of considerable influence in the shaping of the welfare state and its subsequent development. During the 1980s they were also significantly involved in promoting its defence against a government which they believed was not only moving away from consensus politics but running down public services and actively promoting a widening inequality. Conversely,

> Margaret Thatcher and her allies made no secret of their dislike for state employees (with the notable exception of the police and fire services and the armed forces) and of all those occupations dependent for their income on the taxpayer rather than the market. They believed them to be parasitic on the creators of wealth and, undisciplined by market forces, almost by definition inefficient, if not actually incompetent. (Perkin, 1989, p. 486)

This view was bolstered by public choice theory which called into question professional disinterestedness, arguing that professionals had a vested personal interest in state expansion. Part of the Thatcherite project, it has been suggested, was 'to break these entrenched interests and to establish a purged and slimmer, but more objective and impartial state' (Self, 1993, p. 105).

The civil service was also regarded sceptically. 'Informed by experience and their liberal/conservative ideology, Mrs. Thatcher and many of her Party colleagues mistrusted the civil service upon their election and regarded it as a parasitical organisation' (Massey, 1993, p. 30). In fact, the entrenched interests of the civil service have been seen by both incoming Conservative and Labour governments since the war as an obstacle to certain elements of their programme. Mrs Thatcher's reaction was to abolish the Civil Service Department and the Central Policy Review Staff and to develop a programme of 'agencification' (Rhodes, 1997, p. 95). This carried further the process begun in the Heath government of creating separate units of accountable management within government departments, such as the Employment Services Agency (1972) and the Manpower Services Commission (1974). In the 1980s model the primary distinction was between policy and management. While policy remained the responsibility of government departments, operational management increasingly became the responsibility of semi-autonomous agencies. The Social Security Benefits Agency and the Child Support Agency are two well-known examples, but by the end of 1995 there were 109 agencies, employing 67 per cent of the civil service.

If the views of many traditional 'agenda setters' were discounted within the Thatcherite project, new sources of policy initiatives for this ideologically driven government were provided by the right-wing think-tanks that mushroomed in this period. Alongside the long-standing Institute of Economic Affairs, the Adam Smith Institute founded in 1977 and the Centre for Policy Studies established in 1974 extended their influence. 'These bodies provided a vital arena for fusing academic theories with practical policies and for spreading the new gospel among politicians, officials, academics and the media' (Self, 1993, p. 65). While the right-wing think-tanks were 'thinking the unthinkable' (Cockett, 1995), it was not until the late 1980s that there appeared any new equivalent on the Left with the inauguration of the Institute of Public Policy Research.

This section has focussed on some of the features of the Thatcherite hegemony of the 1980s. But, by way of conclusion, two points need to be borne in mind. The first is that 'for much of her premiership Mrs Thatcher sounded more like a leader of the opposition attacking the conventional ideas and institutions of British society' (Pugh, 1994, p. 303). The second is that 'Thatcher's electoral successes did not create a Thatcherite electorate, with 58 per cent voting against her in 1983 and 1987 alike' (Clarke, 1996, p. 388). What impact, then, did Thatcherism have on the classic welfare state?

Thatcherism and the Welfare State

There is general agreement that the Thatcherite project was only extended to the welfare state in her third term of office which began in 1987. There were, of course, earlier initiatives, such as the 1980 Housing Act and the social security reviews instituted in 1984. But the measures introduced after 1987 had 'both novelty and coherence' and 'represented a decision to bring the solvent of market conditions to bear on the problems of the welfare system' (Deakin, 1994, p. 153).

There were many similarities in the policies that were adopted: controlling and reducing the level of public expenditure, stimulating the growth of alternatives to state supply, the introduction of 'opt-outs' and the quasi-market. These were strategies that crossed the boundaries of individual sectors of the welfare state and became part of a more comprehensive approach to welfare reform.

If similar policies were adopted, the pressures for change were diverse. The role of the right-wing think-tanks has already been noted. But there were also more specific influences. Political concern about the escalating costs of residential care for older people was one example. Another was the shaping of the 1990 NHS reforms along the lines of the purchaser/provider split advocated by the American health economist Alain Enthoven. A third, the range of pressures that lay behind the 1988 Education Act and the introduction of the National Curriculum. Each of these, however, were operating within broadly Thatcherite parameters: a concern with costs, a desire to stimulate competition and an attempt to reduce the power of the producer interest. In each case the detail of the reforms was worked out in an environment characterized both by ideology and pragmatism.

This section examines first the local authority welfare state before discussing social security and health. *Conservative government capped the amount of £ local government could earn*

It is impossible to discuss housing and education without referring briefly to the changes which the Conservative governments of the 1980s introduced, controlling the finances and activities of local authorities. Controls on local government spending introduced in the early 1980s were superseded by rate-capping, a tactic designed to penalize those authorities which exceeded levels of spending prescribed by Whitehall. At the same time, new methods of service delivery began to be explored which would have the effect of reducing the role of local authorities. *schools could opt out of local government control + people could buy council houses* Thus schools were to be allowed 'opt-outs' from local authority control, local authority tenants were given the right to buy their council houses, while Social Services Departments were cast in the role of 'enabling authorities' designed to stimulate the widest contribution to care from all the resources of local communities.

The sale of council houses to their tenants had been part of Conservative policy since the late 1950s (Murie, 1975), but it was only with the 1980 Housing Act that tenants were given a statutory 'right to buy' bolstered by significant financial inducements. All tenants of three years' standing were given the right to buy their houses with discounts that began at one-third off the value of the house and rose by 1 per cent for each year of tenancy to a maximum ceiling of 50 per cent discount. 'These were powerful inducements and they produced results

(Glennerster, 1995a, p. 187). Within the decade over 1.2 million council houses were sold, with more than one-sixth of the total stock of council houses sold between 1979 and 1987. The houses that were bought tended to be recently modernized, low-rise properties on 'respectable' estates; those who bought were the more affluent, often two-earner families. The consequence was to further reinforce the role of council housing as a residual sector. By 1986–87 almost two-thirds of local authority tenants were on means-tested benefits (Forrest and Murie, 1988, p. 69); while, as Glennerster (1995a, pp. 187–8) notes, whereas in 1974 just under half the tenants in social housing were in the bottom 40 per cent of the income distribution, by 1991 the proportion was three-quarters, and only 40 per cent of them had jobs. For the Conservatives, the sale of council houses not only represented a slimming of the state, it also reduced Labour's electoral base. 'In the early years especially, the Labour tenants who bought were much more likely to have stopped voting Labour by the time of the next election than those who continued to rent' (Crewe, 1996, p. 410).

In addition to the sale of council houses, there were other facets of the Conservatives' housing programme. First, they followed the pattern of the previous Labour government and concentrated financial support on non-profit housing associations. By the end of the 1980s this had become the main source of supply of new social housing units for lower income rental. Secondly, the Conservatives withdrew the subsidies to local authorities which enabled them to keep down the level of council house rents. Rents were thus brought more into line with those set for housing association and private tenants. And though poorer tenants in all tenures were able to claim means-tested housing benefit, this, in turn, served to push up the social security budget and contributed to the poverty trap (Glennerster, 1995a, p. 186). Thirdly, as the sale of council houses to their individual tenants appeared to be reaching a ceiling, those who continued to rent were given the opportunity to change their landlord (the so-called Tenants' Choice) and Housing Action Trusts were encouraged to take over and improve dilapidated council estates and sell them either to the occupants or another landlord. Both were measures which by-passed the traditional role of the local authority as a supplier and replaced it by 'differentiated service delivery systems' (Rhodes, 1997, p. 125).

Breaking the local authority monopoly and extending parental choice were recurrent features of the Conservatives' education policy during the 1980s. Both these elements featured significantly in the 1988

Education Act, though the foundations of change had already been laid by successive legislation earlier in the decade. Schools were permitted to 'opt-out' of local authority control after a successful ballot of parents and to be financed directly by the Department of Education. Parental choice and the promotion of competition for pupils were encouraged by open enrolment which removed the right of local education authorities to set ceilings on the number of pupils enrolling at a particular school. This removal of local authority control was matched by the introduction of the local management of schools by which budgets were devolved to local schools to be managed by their boards of governors. In addition, school choice was enhanced by the Assisted Places scheme introduced early in the 1980s and the creation of City Technology Colleges funded by a mix of central government finance and private sponsorship.

Responsibility for school and post-school-age education (except for the universities) thus shifted in three dimensions: downwards, to individual schools and colleges and their governors; outwards to parents and other groups (including business interests in the community); and upwards to the Secretary of State (Audit Commission, 1989, pp. 2–3).

The increasing centralisation that characterized educational management in the 1980s, applied most obviously in relation to the National Curriculum. The school curriculum had long been 'a secret garden' controlled by the educational professionals. Callaghan's 1977 Ruskin College speech had challenged that prerogative; and, to a considerable extent, the shape of the National Curriculum, as developed in the 1988 Education Act, was the logical culmination of Callaghan's concern. The National Curriculum not only defined a range of core and additional subjects, it also introduced attainment targets and standardized tests for children at the ages of 7, 11, 14 and 16. The publication of these test scores would, the government believed, provide an important indicator of school performance, while also offering the basic information on which parental choice could be based. Schools were thus being set in competition with each other at the same time as central government control was increasing over the content of the curriculum and the methods of testing and assessment. As Roy Lowe (1997, p. 161) notes:

> central government, despite the claims that schools and parents were being offered greater autonomy, was in reality given greatly enhanced power to control and command the education system. Whether it was

through the determination of funding levels, specific instructions on the curricula, or the control of recruitment numbers, the DES... became, more than ever before the puppeteer of the education system.

The NHS also experienced its 'big bang' (Klein, 1995, p. 176) during Mrs Thatcher's third term of office. Again, there had been earlier and more piecemeal initiatives: increasing centralization replaced delegation and, after Roy Griffiths' 1983 Report, a system of general management was introduced into the NHS in the interests of both increased account-ability and ensuring value for money. Throughout this period, however, public opinion was much more likely to identify with the Labour Party on matters to do with the NHS. The well-publicized leak to *The Economist* in the early 1980s of government plans to substitute private insurance for the tax-funded NHS and to increase charges, led to Mrs Thatcher's much publicized assertion that 'the NHS is safe with us'. It merely underlined the popularity of the NHS and the political danger of creating change that threatened the acknowledged 'jewel in the crown' of the welfare state.

That, however, also changed in the early part of 1988. Despite there being no commitment to NHS change in the 1987 general election manifesto, a ministerial group was established to re-think the NHS and its financing. The memoirs of Margaret Thatcher and Nigel Lawson provide some insight into the process, indicating ideas that were ruled in and ruled out as the discussion proceeded. The result was the White Paper – *Working for Patients* – published in 1989. According to Margaret Thatcher's foreword, its proposals 'represent the most far-reaching reform of the National Health Service in its forty year history' (Cm. 555, HMSO, 1989). Those proposals centred around the creation of an internal market. On the purchasing side would be the district health authorities and those GPs, initially with more than 11 000 patients, who had chosen to hold their own practice budgets. On the supply side, services would be available from a variety of providers: hospitals which remained directly managed by district health authorities (by the early 1990s a small minority), hospital and community units which had opted out of health authority control and become self-governing NHS trusts, private and voluntary suppliers. The link between purchasers and pro-viders was provided by contracts or service agreements setting out prices, treatment levels and quality standards. The creation of the internal market allowed the government to open the NHS to competitive market forces, whilst still continuing the hallowed 'free at the point of use' tax-funded principle.

There were several similarities between the NHS and other reforms that have been considered in this section. These include the opportunity of 'opt-out', devolved budget arrangements and the notion of managed competition in which the purchaser/provider split would operate within guidelines and regulations laid down by central government. This was the 'quasi' (Le Grand and Bartlett, 1993) or 'mimic' (Klein, 1995, p. 184) market in which 'the NHS was to mimic those characteristics of the market that would promote greater efficiency within the framework of a public service committed to the non-market value of distributing access to resources according to need'. That tension has remained part of the story of the NHS in the 1990s.

Social security was also part of the Conservative's restructuring of the welfare state in the 1980s. That is hardly surprising. A government committed to reducing public expenditure inevitably had to concern itself with social security since it formed the largest element of public spending and was its fastest growing sector. The increasing number of older people, the rising incidence of unemployment, and the transfer of housing subsidy from the housing to the social security budget all increased the level of expenditure. Such rising demand threatened the government's wider public spending objectives. Any government's room for manoeuvre, however, is constrained (Heclo and Wildavsky, 1981). In income-maintenance programmes, electoral support – in crude terms, the desire for re-election – as well as the entitlement stake which individuals have acquired in part of the programme, both act as constraints on radical choices. How, then, did the Conservatives endeavour to meet their objectives of reducing public spending, freeing individuals from what they perceived to be the thraldom of state dependency, and creating the conditions for individual reliance and self-help that featured largely in Thatcherism's re-statement of Victorian values?

The first strategy was designed to achieve expenditure reduction. This was done in a variety of ways. The link between the up-rating of National Insurance benefits and wage increases was broken, with price increases being substituted for the latter. The level of child benefit was 'frozen'. This meant that in real terms it lost value. Young people between the ages of 16 and 25 lost some of their entitlements and were paid a lower level of Income Support. There was also a tendency for the value of means-tested benefits to be eroded.

A second strategy was to replace public by private provision. Responsibility for the first eight weeks of sick pay was transferred to employers in 1982. And in the Fowler review of Social Security a proposal was made to abolish SERPS which would have left the responsibility for anything above the basic retirement pension with individuals and employers. As Glennerster (1995a, p. 184) notes, this proposal 'was almost universally opposed, among others by the CBI and the private pensions industry who did not relish having to cater for the low paid with poor job prospects'. The ensuing White Paper preserved SERPS, though the scheme was scaled down in a number of ways (Johnson, 1991, p. 43). Meanwhile 'a stack of rebates and incentives' (Timmins, 1995, p. 402) was introduced to encourage individuals to move from SERPS to their own private pension. By 1993 the cost of this encouragement totalled £9.3 billion in National Insurance rebates and incentives. Another cost was that borne by individuals who 'had succumbed to high pressure salesmanship and been talked into leaving good occupational pension schemes in which they should have stayed' (*ibid.*, p. 403).

Thirdly, there was an increasing emphasis on targeting and administrative simplification. It was somewhat paradoxical that a government concerned to reduce public spending should move more in the direction of means-tested benefits, since they are more costly to administer. The solution lay in simplifying the system, a process already begun by the 1970s review of Supplementary Benefit. Under the Conservatives, Supplementary Benefit was itself re-named Income Support, and the specific additions to an individual's weekly benefit were replaced by a uniform system of premiums. At the same time, Family Income Support was replaced by Family Credit, Housing Benefit conditions were tightened and a more integrated relationship was established between the three principal components of means-tested assistance – Income Support, Family Credit and Housing Benefit. More controversially, the 1986 Social Security Act replaced the entitlement to single payments of the former Supplementary Benefits scheme by a cash-limited Social Fund which provided most of its help through loans reclaimable from weekly benefits:

> From the government's perspective, the Social Fund . . . succeeded in limiting the number of additional payments and thwarting the activities of welfare rights groups. At the same time the replacement of grants by loans and the loss of appeal rights undoubtedly exacerbated the hardship experienced by many claimants. (Deacon, 1995, p. 90)

Financially, the savings represented by the Social Fund were minuscule in the context of the total social security budget. Its symbolic significance was greater. Its creation represented the working out of an agenda set by 'scrounger phobia' in the late 1970s and was an attempt to 'solve' the perceived over-generosity especially of the means-tested part of the social security system. *deserving vs non deserving.*

Overall, Timmins (1995, p. 401) concludes, 'families with children and the elderly gained marginally' from the changes introduced in the 1986 Act, 'at the expense of the unemployed, those without children and particularly those under twenty five'. But comparisons among social security beneficiaries are only part of the story. During the same decade of the 1980s tax cuts were heavily weighted towards the better off, with the richest fifth's share of post-tax and benefit income rising from 40 to 45 per cent, while the poorest fifth's share fell from 6.1 to 5.1 per cent (Peden, 1991, p. 231). It was such evidence that led researchers of the time to highlight 'the growing divide' in British society (Walker and Walker, 1987). This divide had many dimensions. Regionally, the country was divided between the declining North and a buoyant South, in almost a re-run of the economic conditions of the interwar years. But the most fundamental divide was between those in work and those who were unemployed. It was the growing betterment and material improvement of those in work that Margaret Thatcher successfully mobilized in her three election victories. As Peter Clarke (1992, p. 316) observes, 'the great political coup of Thatcherism was not to change human nature but to re-direct it – especially among the skilled working class – away from collect-ive and towards individual gratification'.

The Independent Sector and the Welfare State

During the 1980s the independent sector was increasingly used as a generic term to describe the role of the private market and voluntary organisations in the supply of welfare. How far they were independent of the state is one of the themes to be considered in this section.

There was a certain inevitability about the place accorded to voluntary action in the Thatcherite period. The government was committed to 'rolling back' the frontiers of the state and to restoring Victorian values (Harris, 1992). The nineteenth century had been the age of self-help and mutual aid, of welfare activity predominantly 'outside the state'.

Thatcher wanted to restor victorian values of self help

The Thatcherite project of slimming the state suggested a new (or a rediscovered) role for voluntary activity. But what was that role to be?

As Waine (1992, p. 71) suggests there is both an ambiguity and a changing emphasis in Conservative thinking. This is made clear by a comparison of the statements about the voluntary sector in the 1979 and 1987 Conservative election manifestos. The first proposed that 'We must also encourage the voluntary movement and self-help groups working in partnership with the statutory services'. The latter argued that via tax relief on charitable giving, 'the scope of individual responsibility is widened, the family is strengthened and voluntary bodies flourish. State power is checked'. Whereas, in the earlier statement, the voluntary sector was seen as an addition to state provision – with partnership between them a policy objective – the latter offered a different view: the role of the voluntary sector 'not as a supplement to the state but as an alternative to it' (Finlayson, 1994, p. 359).

That may have been the rhetoric. In practical terms the break with the past was less obvious. Individual donations to voluntary organizations were encouraged in every budget from 1980, and new tax incentives such as payroll-giving and Gift Aid were introduced. Their impact, however, was limited; and throughout the 1980s public finance remained a major source of funding for the voluntary sector. Between 1979 and 1987 it doubled in real terms, fuelled mainly by a continued growth in special employment programmes and by the expansion of funding for the housing associations, whose role in the supply of social housing the government wished to promote. The involvement of the voluntary sector in the Community Programme for unemployed people was especially significant. When it closed in 1988, voluntary agencies were supplying over half the projects of the Programme, while the Manpower Services Commission was providing 20 per cent of all government funding going to the voluntary sector (Deakin, 1995, p. 58). Financial support, however, came at a cost. As Waine (1992, pp. 78–9) notes, 'By their participation in the Community Programme voluntary organisations were providing low-skilled, part-time employment as part of a programme with a definite political bias.' Their involvement thus reduced the independence of the sector as a whole and distorted the work of individual organizations.

In addition to central government, local authorities also provided financial support to the voluntary sector. Many of these were Labour-controlled and funded organizations providing 'political education and equal opportunities for groups who had long been vulnerable to discrimination' (Taylor, 1995, p. 230). Many Conservative MPs were critical of such objectives and of the use of ratepayers' money to fund such organizations. Criticism escalated both in the popular press and in Parliament.

By the end of the decade, however, significant changes had been introduced into the financial support offered by local authorities to the voluntary sector. Compulsory competitive tendering was introduced for a range of local authority services. More specifically, the purchaser/provider changes introduced in the 1990 NHS and Community Care Act replaced fees and grants by the use of contracts specifying a particular form and level of service provision. The climate thus shifted in the direction of 'agreeing prices, defining service and monitoring delivery' (Waine, 1992, p. 81). The implications were considerable. The voluntary sector increasingly faced competition from private care firms, 'floated off' public services reforming as 'not for profits' and NHS trusts. Not only had a more competitive ethos been introduced into the sector. In addition, the survival of smaller organizations often working with less popular clients became a matter of considerable concern, as did the continued support for activities such as advocacy and counselling which lay outside service contracts and arrangements. Meanwhile, in this more market-oriented environment the question was raised (Lewis, 1993, pp. 190–1) of 'how different voluntary organisations will look from public or even private sectors', a question which had already achieved prominence in the United States.

The voluntary sector received ideological support from the Thatcher governments because it operated 'outside the state'. Yet the government stance was paradoxical. Public funds contributed considerably to the financing of voluntary activity and, via contracts and other strategies, the sector became increasingly an agency of the state and subject to more rigorous frameworks of regulation and accountability.

It was equally unsurprising that the Conservative governments of the 1980s supported the role of the private market in welfare. 'If the voluntary sector received the blessing of the New Right, the commercial sector was entirely compatible with its belief in enterprise' (Finlayson, 1994, p. 360). In this sector, too, the government created the conditions for greater use of an extended private provision which was ostensibly 'outside the state'.

Though its importance should not be overestimated, the available evidence suggests that the private sector became a more prominent supplier of welfare during the 1980s. The number of private hospitals increased from 150 to 216, and the number of beds from just over 6500 to almost 11 000. Meanwhile the proportion of the population covered by private health insurance increased from 5 to 9 per cent. Over the same period, the number of children in private education rose from 5.8 to 7.4 per cent (Green and Lucas, 1992). The number of home owners also increased, from 56 per cent at the beginning of the 1980s to 68 per cent at the end of the decade (Goodman, 1997, p. 90). Local authority-provided residential care for older people was increasingly replaced by private sector supply. In pensions, too, as we noted earlier, though SERPS was saved from abolition in the mid-1980s, tax incentives provided a stimulus for individuals to opt for private pension arrangements. By 1993 more than 5 million had opted out of SERPS (Timmins, 1995, p. 403).

The strategies that stimulated private welfare were varied. On the one hand, there was a perception that public services were being run down while, on the other, state provided financial incentives encouraged the expansion of private provision. The popular perception of decline has to be set within the broader context of financial restraint in the public sector. Although resources increased in real terms in the NHS and personal social services and education, they were not sufficient to maintain the former level of service. The issue, therefore, as Wilding (1992, p. 15) argued, was not about 'cuts' but about 'appropriate levels of provision'. This created a perception that 'the whole social welfare enterprise has been run down – or at least those parts of it which depend on direct public expenditure'. That perception, in turn, created a climate in which those who could afford to do so increasingly opted for private provision – whether out of a concern with lengthening waiting lists in NHS hospitals, inadequate textbooks in state schools, or the apparently less generous and tighter controls on state pensions.

Financial incentives underpinned that choice in favour of private provision. Tax reliefs were offered on private health insurance premiums for the over-60s, the Assisted Places scheme offered free places in independent schools to those whose parental income was below a minimum level, and tax incentives were offered to those taking out private pensions. The most significant of the financial incentives, however, were those offered to tenants who wished to buy their council houses. Other incentives also predisposed in favour of private welfare. In the case of the expansion of private residential care, for example, the stimulus was provided by changes to the social security regulations. As a result, social security payments to homes in the private and voluntary sector that had totalled only £10 million in 1979 had increased to £1000 million ten years later. To a very considerable extent, therefore, the state, through the social security system, had underwritten the expansion of private residential care that was one of the most significant changes in personal welfare during the 1980s. In the process it stimulated new suppliers, not least the phenomenon of 'petty bourgeois care': small-scale residential homes often staffed by former nurses (including those who had lost their jobs with the closure of psychiatric and long-stay mental hospitals as part of the community care programme) whose enterprise was legitimated by the ethos of 'family care' (Phillips and Vincent, 1984).

Compared to the doom-laden 'crisis' perspective of the 1970s, in the 1980s 'welfare states...proved resilient in their capacity to command public support, to mobilise resources and to weather economic storms' (Moran, 1988, p. 412). But as this chapter has indicated, change was also a characteristic of the decade. Ideologically, Thatcherism challenged the culture of welfarism, while its legislative programme called into question both the role of traditional suppliers in the state sector and promoted the commercialization of welfare activity (Pierson, 1996, p. 104). Yet paradoxically in this new world of welfare, the state remained 'both large and hyperactive' (Rhodes, 1997, p. 89).

5

GETTING AND SPENDING

> It is an evil, though a necessary one, that the State should have to
> collect and spend a revenue.
>
> (E. Hilton Young, 1924)

Previous chapters have detailed the changing pattern of government responsibility for welfare and the shifting boundaries between the state and other suppliers. The focus so far has been on political, ideological and organizational change. This chapter, by contrast, examines the changing financial arrangements of welfare in the twentieth century, especially in the statutory and voluntary sectors.

At the outset, however, it needs to be remembered that many welfare activities of personal tending care are carried out within families and specifically by women. Much recent research has indicated the financial and the other costs which such personal care entails. In addition, it serves to restrain the costs of welfare provided by the statutory sector by reducing demand.

During the twentieth century an increasing share of government expenditure has been absorbed by welfare activities. This has funded not only the statutory services, but also an increasing share of the welfare activities of local authorities and the voluntary sector as well as subsidizing the private provision of welfare. Not only has the level of public expenditure increased, so too has the incidence of taxation by which to fund it. This chapter, therefore, also looks at the changing pattern of taxation on income, wealth and spending. It ends with a review of some of the available evidence from public opinion studies about popular attitudes to public spending and taxation which have been central issues in recent general election campaigns.

Getting and spending – the raising of resources and their allocation and distribution – is thus integral to the debate about Britain's welfare state. Together they raise questions about whether Britain can continue to afford the solidaristic welfare state of the sort fashioned in the 1940s; while, for other commentators, that welfare state itself has been among the factors blamed for Britain's postwar economic decline.

Public Expenditure: Some Long-Term Trends

In 1996/7 the current level of government spending was £307 billion, a total spend of approximately £5000 per person per year. A large share of this amount is spent on social security (£96.6 billion), health (£42.3 billion), education (£37.8 billion), and social services (£9.8 billion). Spending on employment (£4 billion) and on housing and urban regeneration (£6.4 billion) complete what are usually thought of as the principal welfare activities of government.

Long-term comparisons of expenditure trends are made more difficult by the lack of available data and the changing definitions of included items. Despite such difficulties, general agreement exists about the steady and significant growth in money expenditures and of public expenditure as a proportion of gross domestic product (GDP) during the twentieth century. Peacock and Wiseman's (1967, p. 41) pioneering study estimated total government expenditure at £130.6 million in 1890, £1592 million in 1920 and £6000 million in 1955. As a proportion of gross national product at current prices it increased from 9 per cent in 1890 to 37.5 per cent in 1955. By 1979 it had reached 45.9 per cent of GDP (Middleton, 1996a, p. 91). These figures suggest that for most of this century government expenditure has been on an upward trajectory. For Peacock and Wiseman (1967, p. 52) the pattern over the first half of this century was of 'plateaus of ascending height separated by expenditure peaks' which occurred especially during times of war. Increases in public expenditure, however, have also to be related to rising prices as in the inflationary 1970s, for example, and to the impact of inherited programmes. Between 1945 and 1951, for example, the post-Second World War Labour government introduced 24 new programmes. Over the next 40 years it has been estimated that the impact of those decisions increased expenditure by £7.5 billion (Mullard, 1993, p. 10):

> The inheritance of public policy is the cumulative sum of many actions taken by many governments, each carried forward by the force of political inertia. The greater the momentum behind a programme, the harder it is to slow down, redirect it or stop it. (Rose, 1989, p. 38)

There is general agreement that, especially in the first half of the century, war facilitated the growth of government and of public spending. Wartime conditions generated special additional expenditures on defence, debt repayments and war pensions. But, it has been suggested that they also produced 'a weakening of checks that inhibit the rate of growth of public spending in more normal times' (Peacock and Wiseman, 1967, p. 63). If the Boer War (1899–1902) 'began a revolution in the finances of the state', during the First World War 'the state took responsibility for an ever increasing range of social and economic affairs' (Cronin, 1988, pp. 217–18). Lloyd George's 1914 budget edged towards a total of £200 million, but in 1917 the budget exceeded £2000 million (Clarke 1996, p. 108). During the First World War especially, Treasury control diminished. Several of the new ministries created during the war were not subject to its control; the costs of war-related departments escalated; and at the end of the war Britain's war debt totalled over £1000 million. Such conditions were propitious for a reassertion of Treasury control both over the civil service and public spending, a development that was buttressed by several factors. First, an informal alliance of business interests, Conservatives and many in the middle class who wished to reduce taxation, root out alleged waste in government departments and restrict the role of state activity. Secondly, by the absence of forceful politicians; while those who were forceful like Chamberlain tended to hold orthodox opinions on finance. Thirdly, the greater mobility between government departments which led to 'a cosy homogeneity of opinion in the civil service in which the search for economies was much encouraged' (Crowther, 1988, p. 19).

The Geddes Committee of 1922 and the May Committee of 1931 are the most public and best-known products of those searches for greater economy in public spending. The 'Geddes axe' was wielded over many facets of social expenditure and represented the orthodox belief that 'the budget should be balanced by contraction of government expenditure rather than by increasing revenue through increased taxation which was held to increase business costs and to reduce demand' (Thane, 1996, p. 155). Less than a decade later, the recommendations of the May Committee for total cuts in public spending of £96 million – two-thirds of which were to come from unemployment benefit – brought the second Labour government to an ignominious end in 1931. The subsequent National government raised taxes, cut public salaries and imposed a 10 per cent cut (not the 20 per cent the May Committee had called for) in unemployment benefit.

Despite the emphasis on economy and control of public spending, the amount of social expenditure showed an upward trend. A Treasury White Paper showed an increase from £62.2 million in 1910 to £503.1 million in 1935 (Cmd. 5609). As Dewey notes (1997, p. 68), 'the rise in social spending was much more rapid than that of government spending as a whole, even when allowance has been made for price changes'. Much of the basis for this increasing level of public spending was in place before the First World War with the introduction of old age pensions and the National Insurance scheme. But in the interwar years new programmes were introduced, others extended and the rising levels of unemployment meant that the Treasury had to bear the deficits of the unemployment insurance fund as well as the increasing costs of poor relief. Furthermore, the local authority welfare state was also expanding, and an increasing proportion of its costs was borne by central government.

If the interwar years represented 'creeping collectivism', the years from 1939 to 1979 symbolized 'the consolidation of big government' (Middleton, 1996a). Over that period there was a steady acceleration in public expenditure under all governments – much of it on welfare services – until Labour was forced into severe retrenchment in 1976–77. Once these general trends are disaggregated, some interesting features emerge. First is the steady decline in defence spending: together with the reduction of Britain's imperial commitments, it has been suggested (Judge, 1981, p. 505) that this created 'the fiscal space for the development of the welfare state'. Secondly, within this enlarged fiscal space there was considerable variation in the share of public spending on different services of the welfare state. Between 1951 and 1978 social security accounted for more than 40 per cent of the growth in social expenditure, with the cost of pensions contributing a significant share of the increase. Education and health and personal social services accounted for about 22 per cent. Housing at just over 11 per cent and employment services at almost 3.5 per cent made up the remainder (*ibid*., p. 509). Thirdly, there was considerable variation in party-political support for different welfare programmes. Income maintenance programmes grew more strongly under Labour governments; education tended to be a beneficiary of Conservative governments' spending. Meanwhile, support for public housing tended to be low among the spending priorities of governments of both parties, though it was increasingly residualized after 1980.

As public expenditure levels increased so too did the questioning of whether Britain could afford its welfare state. Correlli Barnett (1986) has forcefully argued that 'the dream of new Jerusalem' represented by the welfare state contributed significantly to Britain's postwar economic decline. His views have been the subject of critical reassessment *inter alia* by Tomlinson and Harris. Discussing Labour's programme of 1945 to 1951 Tomlinson (1997, pp. 261–2) concludes that 'the welfare state ... was an austerity product of an age of austerity' which 'consumed a quite limited level of resources'. Meanwhile Harris (1991, p. 51) has argued that 'there is very little evidence to suggest that welfare state spending got out of control before the mid-1960s'.

Despite such revisionist accounts, there was considerable contemporary concern about the costs of the welfare state. Hence the committees established in the early 1950s – such as Guillebaud and Phillipps – concerned with specific aspects of social expenditure, and the appointment in 1955 of a ministerial Social Services Committee. The context for the Committee's appointment was a concern that 'our social services commitments may run ahead much faster than our resources' (cited in Lowe, 1989, p. 505). Paradoxically, however, rather than agreeing plans to reduce spending as the Treasury wished, 'the Committee provided the opportunity for the consolidation of the defence of welfare state expenditure and for a frontal attack on Treasury assumptions' (*ibid*.). It was thus a crucial moment in 'the replanning of the welfare state' (Lowe, 1996b, p. 255). In the short term it led to the resignation of Thorneycroft as Chancellor of the Exchequer along with other members of the government's Treasury team. In the longer term it led to the establishment of the Public Expenditure Survey Committee (PESC) in 1961. The PESC represented the Conservatives' new-found commitment to planning and was designed to provide a rational means by which the Cabinet might establish spending priorities. This was to be done by matching forecasts for future public expenditure against prospective economic resources. It is the more incongruous, therefore, that the PESC by the mid-1970s had become not a vehicle 'for the control but for an explosion of public expenditure which forced the then Labour government to introduce cash limits and drastically to reduce, in real terms, for the only time in post-war history, both public and welfare expenditure' (Lowe, 1997, p. 467).

Public expenditure 'cuts' thus pre-date Thatcher and the Conservative governments of the 1980s. But an early White Paper gave an indication of their analysis. It was public expenditure that 'lay at the heart of Britain's economic difficulties' (Cmnd. 7746, p. 1). The Thatcherite project was thus concerned to combat the effects of an inflated public sector which

> had led to high taxes and . . . contributed to disincentives to work and to invest; to social malaise by creating larger numbers of dependants on the public sector; and to increased expectations which government could not realise. (Butcher, 1990, p. 57)

The medicine was strong and varied (Thain and Wright, 1990). Cash planning targets and cash limits set by central government were introduced; new controls were imposed on local authority finances; new techniques for achieving efficiency and value for money were introduced into the public sector in the form of Compulsory Competitive Tendering, new management systems and the break up of the state monopoly in the welfare sector. Yet despite such efforts the Conservative governments of the 1980s made little impact either on the level of public expenditure or on the burden of taxation. The effect of the two prolonged depressions since 1979 and the failure to achieve real cuts in social expenditure produced the situation in which the *ex ante* public expenditure planning total in 1993/4 was 1.5 percentage points above that inherited by the Conservative in 1979 (Middleton, 1996b, p. 143).

Demand-side factors undoubtedly contributed to that outcome. The return to levels of unemployment that had not been experienced since the 1930s and the ageing of the population both worked against the government's financial aspirations. But demands on the Exchequer were also the result of changes in supply. Portable pensions, for example, were given substantial tax advantages while charitable donations by companies and individuals were made the subject of tax subsidies. As a result the pressures increased on public expenditure and there occurred a blurring of the distinction between the public and the private sectors.

Issues of public spending, of course, go beyond the macro perspective that has been presented in this section. Slicing the cake of public resources between spending programmes (not all of them concerned with welfare) is only the first stage. Ensuring that resources meet needs and provide the means to deliver an effective and efficient service is another and important aspect of the politics of public expenditure (see Glennerster, 1992a, Part II). Underpinning both macro- and micro-level decisions, however, is the issue of raising revenue.

Raising Revenue

Governments have a variety of revenue-raising methods at their disposal: borrowing, the receipts from the sale of public assets and the revenue raised by North Sea Oil are three examples. But throughout this century taxation of income, wealth and spending has been a central means of raising revenue. Over that period three main trends can be discerned. The number of taxes has increased and so too has the number of people who are required to pay them. Secondly, National Insurance contributions and value added tax, the successor to purchase tax, have contributed an increasing proportion of government revenue, the latter especially since 1979. Thirdly, though taxes on capital have also increased, there has been a lack of enthusiasm to move towards a wealth tax, though it has had powerful advocates at specific periods (Whiting, 1996, ch. 7).

Two features of the modern taxation system were already in place at the beginning of the century. These were income tax and the tax levied on the transfer of assets after death. Income tax was first levied as a temporary expedient at the end of the eighteenth century, and was re-introduced by Peel in 1842 ostensibly to combat the budget deficit. For much of the nineteenth century there was considerable political unanimity that its rate should be kept low and that it should be repealed when possible. Before the end of the century, however, it had already begun its upward trajectory. According to Middleton (1996a, p. 203) 'measured as the net produce per (old) penny of standard rate, the yield of the British income tax rose progressively from £2142 million in 1889/90 to £3109 million in 1913/14'. In addition to income tax, estate duty was introduced in 1889 and superseded by graduated death duties in 1894. Initially levied at 8 per cent on estates valued at over £1 million, it

provoked considerable opposition among the aristocracy. Oscar Wilde
gave to Lady Bracknell in *The Importance of Being Earnest*, first per-
formed in 1895, its most famous condemnation:

> What between the duties expected of one during one's lifetime and
> the duties exacted from one after one's death, land has ceased to be
> either a profit or a pleasure.

In the first decade of the century, however, it was by no means certain
that class-based taxation was to be the means of financing an expanding
state and its growing social and defence commitments. At that time tariff
reform – strongly advocated by Joseph Chamberlain in his bid to lead
the Conservative Party – appeared a significant alternative. It had two
advantages. On the one hand, it represented a means of protecting
Britain's manufacturing industry and hence jobs against foreign competition. On the other, levying import duties would generate revenue
that could be used for the purposes of social reform. As a tax on
consumption, tariffs would 'spread the burden of increased taxation
across all of society, thereby avoiding paying for social reform through
openly class-biased taxation' (Green, 1996, pp. 236–7). As a tax on
consumption, however, it also threatened the living standards of many
British households by levying a tax on foreign imported foodstuffs: an
argument symbolized by the Liberal's campaign which contrasted the
'little loaf' of tariff reform with the 'big loaf' of free trade. As Green
points out (1995, p. 3), 'in an electoral system dominated by low earners
the Conservatives appeared to be threatening to raise the cost of living,
and three general election defeats provide strong prima facie evidence
that the Conservatives paid a heavy price for their advocacy of "food
taxes"'.

The Liberal's alternative – that of direct taxation – was embodied in
Lloyd George's 'People's' Budget in 1909 which introduced a new
supertax on the very rich and a graduated and differentiated system
of taxes on income. In addition, the duty was increased on beer, spirits
and tobacco and taxes were introduced on new trends in consumer
expenditure, such as motoring. Most controversial were the land value
duties which the budget proposed. For Lloyd George himself it was 'a
War Budget. It is for raising money to wage implacable warfare against
poverty and squalidness' (cited in Fraser, 1984, p. 157). Many features of
the 1909 budget had, however, been presaged in Asquith's budget of
1907 and even after 1909 the numbers of those subject to income and

capital taxes remained small. Middleton (1996a, p. 204) notes that in 1914/15 they totalled 1.24 million, with only 0.164 million paying income tax at the top rate.

The significance of the 1909 budget was two-fold. On the one hand, it established the interrelationship between public finance and social policy. On the other, it affirmed that taxation ought to be related to ability to pay. This principle was reflected 'both in the system of graduation and in the shift from indirect taxes on consumption . . . to direct taxes on income and wealth' (Pugh, 1994, p. 118). As such the taxation system became redistributive, even if the level of redistribution achieved was modest; and it fostered a widespread acceptance that the system of central government taxation was equitable. As a result, Daunton (1996a, p. 15) has suggested that there was a greater willingness to rely on tax-funded welfare schemes in Britain compared to other European countries.

Despite the growing political reliance on taxation, however, the system of National Insurance introduced in 1911 provided another means of financing increased welfare commitments. Health and unemployment benefits were to be paid for by compulsory contributions levied on employers and workers with a supplementary contribution paid by the Treasury. Four influences can be discerned in the evolution of national insurance. First, the place of insurance in the traditions of working-class self-help and mutual aid. Second, Lloyd George's visit to Germany in 1908 where he saw the operation of the scheme of social insurance introduced by Bismarck in the early 1880s. Third, the politically expedient use of national insurance as an alternative to the entrenched positions of the Majority and Minority Reports on the Poor Laws which reported in 1909. Fourth, the reaction to the introduction of non-contributory and tax-funded old age pensions which had considerably exceeded the estimates of initial expenditure. For the purposes of continuing 'the battle against poverty and squalidness' and extending welfare services 'insurance by drawing on the funds of workers and their employers, could provide the necessary resources' (Fraser, 1984, p. 162).

Wartime demands brought taxation to the centre of the political stage after 1914. Despite the fact that politicians were fearful of the effects of high levels of taxation and consciously attempted to restrict taxation to what was thought necessary to cover the cost of wartime borrowing, maximum tax rates rose from 12.5 per cent to 52 per cent during the war (Lawrence, 1994, p. 154). Rates of taxation which had risen during the war years did not revert to their former levels afterwards. In the interwar years they never fell below 4s (20p) in the pound. In addition, income tax was made more progressive and, since the thresholds at which levels of taxation became payable failed to keep pace with inflation, more of the population became taxpayers. Similarly, the number of supertax and surtax payers increased, and their tax rates became more steeply progressive (Dewey, 1997, p. 63). Throughout the period there was greater emphasis on direct taxation compared to taxes on consumption, though duties on beer and tobacco tended to adversely effect working-class living standards.

The need for revenue during the Second World War produced a situation similar to that of 1914–18: tax rates rose, personal allowances were reduced and the scope of purchase tax introduced in 1940 was extended. In addition, administrative arrangements changed. PAYE was introduced in 1943 by which tax was automatically deducted from wages and salaries during the course of the year. Over the period of the war, government revenue increased from £980 million in 1939 to £3265 million in 1945, while the contribution of direct taxation rose from 52 to 63 per cent (*ibid.*, p. 285). Meanwhile, the reduction of personal allowances altered the profile of taxpayers, bringing more working-class taxpayers into the system. Yet even the largely increased wartime tax yield did not fund the total of government spending. Expenditure outstripped receipts; the shortfall being made up by government borrowing, the land-lease agreement and the Marshall Aid programme. There can be little doubt, however, that the larger tax-take necessitated by the war created a popular legitimation of taxation revenue that was to be 'vital in providing the taxable capacity for carrying into effect the post-war settlement' (Middleton, 1996a, p. 489).

In the immediate postwar period the Attlee government retained the steeply progressive wartime tax structure, increased the incidence and rate of surtax and raised the rate of death duties on estates over £12 500. By the end of the decade, however, Labour's approach was generating increasing concern, not least among some of its own supporters. There were two dimensions to the argument. First, that high levels of taxation were a threat to investment. Secondly, in the light of year-on-year increases in social spending, there were some who wondered whether Britain was reaching the level of taxable capacity. These were issues which the Labour government remitted to a Royal Commission on the Taxation of Profits and Incomes. Before it reported in 1955, however, the context had changed. The Conservatives were back in power; the

Korean War, that had necessitated Gaitskell's rearmament budget in 1950, was over; and world trade prices had begun to move in Britain's favour. This enabled the Conservatives to redeem their 1945 election pledge to make 'an early reduction in taxation' and to reward those – especially their middle-class supporters – who had returned to the Conservative Party at the 1950 and 1951 general elections. According to Cronin (1991, p. 208), however, the politicians' tax-cutting agenda vied with 'the logic of fiscal responsibility'. This appealed especially to government officials and to the City, and gave priority to expenditure cuts over lower taxes. Hence the pattern of successive budgets during the 1950s which endeavoured to satisfy both constituencies by offering minor tax concessions while restraining government spending.

As a result, the proportion of taxation to GNP was at a low postwar level at the end of the 1950s. By 1970 it had increased from 28.4 per cent to over 44 per cent. Those figures indicate that it was the 1960s which witnessed the 'take off' in social expenditure as the 'spartan, minimalist and safety net character' of the Beveridgean welfare state adapted to 'the values and aspirations of a more affluent and millenarian age' (Harris, 1991, p. 52). This changing context had its impact on taxation. Conservatives raised indirect taxes in the 1960s: Labour, in government later in the decade, introduced new ones: capital gains tax, corporation tax and selective employment tax. The major change in taxation during the 1960s and 1970s, however, occurred as the result of inflation. Not only did it automatically push taxation up in line with prices

> but in a process that has been termed 'fiscal drag' it actually increased the liability of ordinary workers to income tax [and] lifted many lower-middle-class incomes into higher rates of tax and thus took a bigger share of most incomes. (Cronin, 1991, p. 241)

The result was mounting opposition to the taxing state and increased popular support for the Conservatives' 1979 election commitment to reduce public expenditure and lower the tax burden. The political legitimacy accorded to high taxation and a proactive state in the 1940s appeared to have been broken. The political discourse of the later 1970s was structured around the disincentives of the tax system and its stultifying effect on manufacturing investment. Meanwhile, the popular image was of wasteful expenditure on a welfare state that had grown uncontrollably, an image reinforced by often unsubstantiated allegations of social security benefit fraud in the popular press.

The Conservatives tax-cutting agenda, therefore, had considerable popular appeal; but it can hardly be judged successful. 'Taxation accounted for 38.5 per cent of GDP in 1979 and 40.75 in 1990' (Evans, 1997, p. 31). The crucial difference between those dates, however, lay in the nature of the taxation burden. Direct taxation, whose share of government revenue had increased from 57 to over 75 per cent between 1970 and 1975, was reduced; indirect taxation rose. Reductions in the Conservatives' first budget in the higher and standard rates of income tax were followed later in the 1980s by the simplifying of the tax system into two bands, a standard rate of 25 per cent and single higher rate of 40 per cent. Measures such as these reinforced the ideological thrust towards rewards for initiative, enterprise and hard work that were the hallmarks of Thatcherite populism. Meanwhile, raising the level of value added tax (the replacement of purchase tax) introduced in 1973, extending its provisions and introducing other indirect taxes signalled a switch to expenditure-based taxation. Together with the withdrawal of the Treasury subsidy which made National Insurance contributions a tax in all but name, it created a more regressive tax system and exacerbated the growing inequalities that characterized the 1980s.

Its legacy in the 1990s has been to establish an apparent political consensus centred on controlling public expenditure and levels of taxation. How far this reflects public attitudes will be discussed in a later section. But Hills (1996a, p. 93) has argued that, while 'the options for tax policy remain wide open', discussion of those options 'needs to be less divorced from the reason why taxation is there – the need to raise revenue to finance public spending in the fairest and most efficient way'.

He who Pays the Piper...

The next sections look at the local authority welfare state and the voluntary sector. In both of them during the twentieth century central government funding has become more predominant. That change in financial arrangements has reduced the autonomy of both sectors and increased the control of central government. He who pays the piper has increasingly called the tune.

Local Welfare, Central Finance

During the twentieth century many public welfare services have been supplied by units of local government. Education, public housing and personal welfare are well-known examples. That pattern of local delivery had its origins in the local administration of poor relief inaugurated in the sixteenth century: but it was considerably extended during the nineteenth century in sectors such as public health, environmental services and elementary education. A traditional system of local rates levied on property had been the means of financing the Poor Law. But as responsibilities increased during the nineteenth century, specific grants were paid from central government to local agencies. These included the grant to schools based on attendance and examination successes, the so-called 'payment by results' scheme of 1862. In 1888 such individual grants totalling just over £4 million, compared to the local authorities' rate income of £22 million, were replaced by revenues assigned by central government with local discretion over how they would be spent.

In practice, however, the assigned revenues 'proved insufficiently elastic to keep pace with local spending' (Bellamy, 1988, p. 52) which increased from £27.3 million to £48.2 million between 1870 and 1890, and had risen to £125.8 million by 1910. Such an increase evoked considerable opposition from ratepayers' organizations (McCord, 1978), and by the end of the nineteenth century there was 'increasing political conflict over provision of local services and growing demands for retrenchment and for relief to local authorities from the national exchequer' (Harris, 1993, p. 201). That relief came in two forms. The first was national taxation that would shift the responsibility for social policy away from local and on to central government. This was especially marked in the New Liberals pre-First World War social programme, based upon the twin pillars of direct taxation and National Insurance. The second, which was also introduced before the First World War, was a return to the payment of central government grants to fund specific aspects of local government activity.

During the interwar years local government took on additional responsibilities and was an important supplier of education, housing, public health and the financial support of those not covered by the National Insurance scheme. The last was especially important in the economic depression of the 1920s and 1930s. Increasing responsibilities meant that expenditure increased. Between 1913 and 1939 total local authority spending rose from £140 million to £553 million, with much of the increase attributable to welfare spending (Stevenson, 1984, p. 308). Over the same period income from rates and local authority borrowing increased. But an increasing share of local government expenditure was met by grants from central government. Central government grants in aid of revenue expenditure, for example, more than doubled between 1920 and 1930 (Young, 1985, p. 8). As subsidies from central government increased, so 'local authorities drifted towards merely implementing its policies' (Harrison, 1996, p. 119), a strategy highlighted by central government's attempt to restrain certain elements of local authority spending in the aftermath of the 1931 financial crisis. Many of the contributors to *A Century of Municipal Progress* published in 1935 used the opportunity presented by the centenary of the Municipal Corporations Act to assert the values of local government and to highlight the threats of centralization (Laski, 1935; see also Robson, 1933).

But it was a lament for a world that was passing. As Crowther (1988, p. 47) notes, 'the economic problems of the time encouraged central control, since local authorities in the depressed areas were in a constant state of financial crisis'. Meanwhile, Neville Chamberlain's quest for administrative efficiency embodied in the 1929 Local Government Act had further reinforced the tendency towards centralization. The Act again attempted to replace individual grants by a block grant to local authorities, altered local government tax boundaries, de-rated agricultural land entirely and relieved 'productive' industry of 75 per cent of its local rate liability, and offered local authorities financial compensation for their loss of revenue (Gilbert, 1970, p. 230).

The financial arrangements established during the interwar years became an ongoing feature of the central–local government partnership that characterized the 'classic' welfare state over the 30 years from the mid-1940s. Central government grants increased from 30 per cent at the end of the Second World War to 47 per cent in 1976, while over the same period, as a proportion of total public expenditure, local authority spending increased from 25 per cent to almost one-third. Perhaps even more significant is the fact that by the end of the 1970s domestic rates were financing less than 20 per cent of the cost of local government spending. Industry, commerce and especially central government were by that time the principal revenue providers (Jackman, 1985, p. 157).

Domestic rates were thus back on the political agenda; so too from the mid-1970s were political concerns about the rising proportion of local authority spending. Under Labour there were 'drastic cuts in capital programmes and reversal of ambitious long-term plans for expansion of services' (Deakin, 1985, p. 221). The Conservative measures were more radical: the abolition of what were perceived to be high spending authorities such as the Greater London Council and the metropolitan county councils; the establishment of an Audit Commission to oversee local authority finances; the reduction in the central government grant ; the introduction of measures to prevent local authorities seeking a supplementary rate, and powers enabling the Secretary of State for the Environment to 'cap' the rates of overspending councils. Each of these measures represented a new configuration in the relations between central and local government.

It was the Conservative proposals for changing the method of local finance, however, that generated the most political controversy. A Green Paper published in 1986 – *Paying for Local Government* – proposed extensive changes involving both domestic and commercial ratepayers. The plan was to replace the latter by a national non-domestic rate, while domestic rates levied on property values were to be replaced by a flat-rate poll tax or community charge levied on practically all adults at levels set by the local authority. To its supporters, the community charge had the value of making more transparent the spending pattern of each local authority and of providing a basis for paying for local services that was more inclusive than the rating system had been. To its opponents, it represented a regressive tax to be paid at a pre-determined level irrespective of income, wealth or housing status. The infamous 'poll tax riots' contributed to the downfall of Margaret Thatcher as Prime Minister, and one of the early decisions of her successor John Major's government was to replace the community charge by a new council tax. Like its predecessor, the council tax took account of the number of adults in a household; but, like the rating system, it was based on the value of property within one of eight broad bands.

At the end of the century the position is the reverse of what it was at the beginning: only a small proportion of local government spending is financed by locally variable taxes. That raises issues of democratic accountability, but it also highlights the changing balance of power in central–local government relations.

Mutual Aid, Charity and Contract

Much the same pattern is discernible in the voluntary sector: that amalgam of self-help and mutual aid organizations and the tradition of philanthropic and charitable activity. Common to both, however, is a changing financial relationship which led ultimately to the demise of the former and a significant increase in state-funding for the latter.

Friendly Societies were the principal agencies of mutual aid at the beginning of the century. Membership was open to those who were able to afford the regular contributions and to meet the minimum wage clause which some of the societies imposed. In return, members became part of a social fellowship organized around regular club nights and were able to claim sickness benefit on a sliding scale and a sum to cover the cost of funeral expenses.

From their membership peak at the start of the century, the societies began a relative decline. Though the membership of those societies offering a full range of sickness services increased from 4.1 million in 1901 to 4.5 million in 1931, as a proportion of the adult male population coverage declined from more than 40 per cent to less than one-third over the same period. It is tempting to see this as a direct consequence of the expansion of state provided welfare services. Daunton (1996a, p. 13) has suggested that other factors also need to be taken into consideration, not least the societies' own financial problems.

At the beginning of the century those problems centred around membership. Societies were increasingly competing for members and there were a growing number of older members to whom long-term sickness benefits were paid as an incipient old age pension. The societies thus faced a dilemma. On the one hand, the competition for new members made it difficult to increase their subscriptions or reduce their benefit levels. On the other, the ageing constituency increased demands on their funds (Finlayson, 1994, p. 138). It has been suggested (Johnson, 1996, p. 234) that this was one of the reasons why their opposition to state old age pensions was so muted.

The competition was not only for new members. It was also, after 1911, between the Friendly Societies and the commercial insurance companies such as the Pearl and the Prudential who had also been accorded the title of Approved Societies in the National Insurance Act. As a result the Friendly Societies faced 'competition from highly profitable and aggressive concerns' (Daunton, 1996b, p. 182) in the field of sickness insurance. By 1922, of the 2208 societies granted the status of

Approved Societies, 1192 had ceased to operate under the terms of the 1911 Act. Those which survived tended to be the larger collecting Friendly Societies and the commercial insurance companies, both of which had benefited by holding larger funds and by the high postwar interest rates. During the depression years of the interwar period, central government increased its control over the supposedly autonomous Friendly Societies, reducing its subvention so that 'reserves were eroded and profits were in effect diverted to the Exchequer' (Daunton, 1996b, p. 185).

This growing intervention was taken one stage further in the Beveridge Report which envisaged the state acting as a single Approved Society for the nation. Beveridge himself saw a continuing role for the societies at least in sickness insurance despite the fact that their coverage was far from comprehensive (Cmd. 6404, para. 379). The Labour government, however, abolished their involvement in its National Insurance scheme. As Finlayson (1994, p. 270) points out, 'the Approved Societies finally fell victim to the argument that only the state could in the interests of universality and should in the interests of equity undertake such matters'. Such a conclusion was also the culmination of a long-standing Labour concern about the lack of direct accountability of the commercial insurance companies. 'The fact that the Approved Societies had bolted into the stable of the bureaucratic and unaccountable commercial companies weakened the case for reliance on non-state organisations' (Daunton, 1996b, p. 184). Labour's more comprehensive state insurance system, therefore, left no formal place for the voluntary tradition, with few voices 'raised from within their ranks against the obliteration of the last vestiges of direct popular control over the relief of poverty' (Vincent, 1991, pp. 128–9).

The extension of state responsibility also created a new terrain for the philanthropic tradition in voluntary activity; though, like the Approved Societies, its sources of finance were also changing before the inauguration of the 'classic' welfare state in the 1940s.

Already by the beginning of the century there was expression of concern about the continuing viability of the philanthropic sector. In the rural areas the agricultural depression had depleted the resources of the landowners for philanthropic purposes; while the annual subscriber, who had been the mainstay of much nineteenth-century charity, was increasingly regarded as a precarious source of income.

Despite these concerns the philanthropic tradition 'showed continued vitality' (Stevenson, 1984, p. 314) in the interwar years. Constance

Braithwaite's (1938, p. 168) contemporary study estimated the income of charitable organizations in England and Wales at between £35 million and £50 million. Her study also highlighted dimensions of change. First, a decline in bequests from large estates had been offset by 'an increasing flow from estates in the medium category'. Secondly, the apparent steadiness of charitable income was insufficient to keep pace with rising prices. Thirdly, voluntary donations represented a declining proportion of charitable income. By contrast, payments by local authorities to voluntary organizations for services which they provided were becoming increasingly important. This constituted what Elizabeth Macadam (1934) termed 'the new philanthropy' and it continued to characterize the voluntary sector in the post-Second World War period.

Studies in the 1970s (for example Falush, 1977) showed a decline both in personal and company-giving to voluntary organizations, while the level of subvention from central government and local authorities continued to increase, a trend highlighted by research undertaken for the Wolfendon Committee (1978). Such financial support helped the voluntary sector to offset its diminishing traditional sources of revenue. It also created a crisis of identity. How far was it – or could it be – independent of the state and, where necessary critical of it, when an increasing proportion of its revenue came from government sources?

The Conservative governments of the 1980s made much in their rhetoric of the contribution of the voluntary sector. But they believed that it 'must look largely to the charity of individuals for financial support' (Patrick Jenkin cited in Brenton, 1985, p. 68). Meanwhile, as a result of central government-imposed spending limits many voluntary organizations experienced a real reduction in their level of support both from central government departments and local authorities.

It was thus against the background of a quest for autonomy and a harsher financial climate that the voluntary sector embarked upon the search for new methods of financing its activities. Charity shops, targeted mail shots, the Christmas card business and special appeals such as Children in Need are some examples of that initiative. Yet, paradoxically, the principal source of funding for the voluntary sector since 1990 has been the contribution of fees and charges paid to the sector by local authorities on the basis of a social care contract established between them. The introduction of the 'contract culture' by the 1990 NHS and Community Care Act has thus brought the voluntary sector full circle to the financial position established in the interwar years. But, as several assessments have noted, its recent manifestation creates an uncertain future for the voluntary sector:

> in future many voluntary organisations may be in competition not merely with each other but also with for-profit commercial organisa- tions. This, in turn, will raise questions about the definition and legal and fiscal privileges of voluntary organisations. (Leat, 1995, p. 184)

Tax and Spend and Public Opinion

At the beginning of the century working-class people regarded state welfare as a poor substitute for full employment (Thane, 1984), and even in the 1940s 'there was no evidence to suggest that grassroots opinion was harbouring any wider vision of a more far reaching social revolution' of the sort Beveridge proposed (Harris, 1983b, p. 214). The institutionalization of the welfare state appears to have brought about a change in public opinion. Even over the past two decades, when it could be argued that the welfare state has lost some of its popular legitimacy, analysts have shown a remarkable consistency in public support. *The British Social Attitudes* longitudinal survey in fact showed evidence of growing support for increased spending on welfare services in the decade between 1983 and 1993, with a decline among those in favour of reducing taxes and spending less (Taylor-Gooby, 1995, p. 3).

Increasingly, however, surveys of public opinion have disaggregated the general picture. When that is done by service sector there is a considerable variation in public support. Services for the elderly, the sick and disabled, education and the NHS tend to have strong support. Public opinion is, however, 'more antipathetic to benefits for the unem- ployed, low paid, lone parents and children, with other services occupy- ing an intermediate position' (Taylor-Gooby, 1985, p. 29). Interestingly, such variation in public support tends to preserve the distinction made in earlier times between the deserving and the undeserving.

The NHS, education and pensions regularly feature as those services on which the public would like to see increased spending (Taylor-Gooby, 1995, pp. 3–4). Such a response, however, comes not only from those who use public services, but also from those who have private health

insurance or whose children are at school in the private sector (Brook
et al., 1996, p. 198).

A further feature of the growing sophistication of public opinion
surveys has been the juxtaposition of items designed to explore the
relationship between spending programmes and taxation. An early
study in the 1960s (Butler and Stokes, 1974, p. 459) indicated increasing
support for tax cuts and a decline in those supporting increased welfare
spending: the nucleus, in other words, of popular support for the
Thatcherite agenda. More recent evidence in the 1980s and 1990s,
however, has shown increased support for higher welfare spending
and an in-principle agreement to pay more through taxation to fund
it. *The British Social Attitudes* survey also indicates considerable unanimity
about where that tax burden ought to fall:

> the majority...believes that those on low incomes are paying too
> much and those on high incomes too little...The public mood
> would thus seem to endorse a more progressive tax strategy than is
> currently in place. (Taylor-Gooby, 1995, p. 13)

The issue of tax remains a sensitive matter to both the main political
parties, as recent history suggests. The Conservative's 'double whammy'
attack on Labour during the 1992 general election campaign was coun-
terbalanced by Labour's publicity of Conservative tax rises in the years
after 1992, and Labour's own commitment in the 1997 election both to
maintain the previous government's spending limits and not to raise
any income tax rates. Given that there is evidence suggesting that a
majority favour higher welfare spending and higher taxes, recent studies have begun to explore what motivates such an opinion. The answer
at present appears ambivalent, reflecting a mixture both of self-interest
and a wider public concern that can be thought of as the national
interest (Lipsey, 1994, p. 202). Health and education, for example,
tend to be perceived both as a private benefit (self-interest) and a public
good (national interest) (Brook *et al.*, 1996, p. 189).

It is well-established that individuals may behave differently from the
replies they give in opinion surveys, and that factors other than issues of
taxation and welfare spending may influence their political choice.
None the less, the evidence reviewed in this section suggests that at
the end of the twentieth century there appears to be a desire to maintain
and expand – and pay for – services such as health and education. But
there are other sectors of the welfare state – those directed specifically at

the disadvantaged minority – which do not command the same level of public support. 'Although the contented majority may not have turned its back on the welfare state, it is far from clear that it would tolerate a redirection to the greater benefit of an increasingly excluded minority' (Taylor-Gooby, 1995, p. 6). Tax and spend, therefore, appear to operate within narrow parameters at the end of the century in which they have dominated political action and debate.

6

PROFESSIONALS, MANAGERS AND USERS

We all disliked the do-good volunteer and wanted to see him replaced by professionals and trained administrators in the socialist welfare state of which we all dreamed.

(R.H.S. Crossman, 1976, pp. 64–5)

The welfare state is not only a distributive mechanism of benefits and services. Over the course of the past century the state – and especially the welfare state – has been a major employer. It has thus contributed to the changing profile of the British labour force, not least in the employment opportunities it has offered to women. But in the opinion especially of its right-wing critics, it has done more. It has established a vested interest of those whose defence of the welfare state has been based less on a commitment to the services it offers to users, and more as a means of self-interestedly preserving their own employment.

Those same services have increasingly been supplied by trained professionals and administrators; and it has been a recurring theme in the literature on the welfare state that – to slightly paraphrase Douglas Jay (1937, p. 317) – the men in Whitehall or the town hall knew what was best for the well-being of the national or local population. A welfare state that gave preeminence to professionally-defined needs and ways of meeting them, inevitably assigned a more peripheral position to consumers and users. The chapter ends, therefore, by discussing the related and more recent themes of the challenge to professional power, the new managerialism and the rise of the consumer interest.

The Changing Labour Force

Three long-term trends characterize the changing labour force of the twentieth century. First, the decline in manufacturing industry and the growth of the service sector. Secondly, the expansion of public sector employment. Finally, the increased participation of women in paid employment, both full and part time. Each of these trends is to some degree interrelated; all of them bear upon the welfare state as an employer.

Manufacturing Decline, Service Sector Growth

The proportion of the workforce engaged in manufacturing reached its peak in 1914 and declined thereafter. Increasing international competitiveness challenged Britain's supremacy as the 'workshop of the world', and it was especially those regions which had been at the forefront of industrial activity in the nineteenth century which most severely experienced the onset of depression in the interwar years. At that time 'towns in Lancashire, South Wales, Tyneside, lowland Scotland, the heartlands of the classical industrial revolution, experienced levels of unemployment up to 70 per cent of the workforce' (Overy, 1988, p. 43). At the same time, however, there was a considerable expansion in new industries such as motor car manufacture and light engineering which were concentrated in southern England and the Midlands. The long-term pattern that has characterized the twentieth century, however, was established; although even in the mid-1960s production industries still accounted for just under half of total employment. Thereafter, decline was much more rapid. Between 1966 and 1988 the numbers employed in manufacturing declined from 8.7 million to 5 million workers, 2 million manufacturing jobs being lost during the 1980s alone (McDowell, 1988, p. 141). This represented a major structural change in Britain's employment profile, and occasioned a huge debate on de-industrialization.

Contemporaneously with the decline in manufacturing industry, there has been an expansion of the service sector. By the late 1980s, 14 million people were employed in service occupations (McDowell, *ibid*.). Such jobs were principally concentrated in insurance, banking, financial and business services and in public, professional and scientific services. The beginnings of a sustained 'take off' in both these sectors occurred during the interwar period and immediately following the

Second World War. The rising real wages of those in work stimulated increased consumer consumption and a retailing revolution, while the expansion of local government services and the insurance and financial sectors showed an increase in employment of 30 per cent or more in the years between 1920 and 1938 (Feinstein, 1972, table 59). Meanwhile the postwar period was characterized especially by the expansion of administrative, managerial and professional occupations.

Together, the changes in manufacturing industry and the service sector have transformed the profile of Britain's labour force over the course of this century. From overwhelmingly 'blue collar' at its beginning, it is now predominantly 'white collar' and 'white blouse', a recognition that the majority of jobs for both men and women are now located in service industries.

There are at least three ways in which the changes that have just been reviewed have impacted upon the welfare state. First, the much highlighted regional dimension in the transformation between manufacturing industry and the service sector influenced the role which governments from the 1930s assumed in what was termed 'the regional problem'. From that time state intervention was not only about the consequences of economic dislocation for individuals, it was also concerned with regional economic imbalance. Over the past 60 years a variety of regional policies have been introduced. These have included the designation of Special Area status, control over industrial location, premiums and incentives to encourage investment and, more recently, the development of public/private corporations and partnerships to stimulate economic revival and prosperity.

The second issue concerns social mobility. Several writers have argued that the increase in non-manual occupations that has taken place this century should have broken the chain of working-class sons and daughters following their parents into manual 'blue collar' occupations. While Goldthorpe's (1980) research indicated a substantial amount of social mobility, it also revealed that the tendency to avoid manual labour was even greater amongst the sons of non-manual fathers. The higher socio-economic groups have thus benefited more from the changes in employment structure than their working-class counterparts.

Thirdly, the expansion of the service sector was used by Bacon and Eltis (1978) in an influential analysis in the mid-1970s to highlight the threat to Britain's industrial and manufacturing base and to long-term prosperity. Since the welfare state had itself been a major contributor to service employment, their analysis became part of the growing critique of the welfare state at that period, highlighting the discontinuity between the so-called 'burden' of welfare and the productive nature of manufacturing industry and investment.

The Growth of Public Sector Employment

Middleton (1996a, p. 106) indicates that the public sector's share of the total working population increased nearly eight-fold between 1891 and 1979, rising from 3.6 per cent to 27.9 per cent. As such it constitutes a 'crude indicator of the growing role of the state' (Johnson, 1994b, p. 477). Considerable care, however, is needed in interpreting the available statistics. Public sector employment represents an amalgam of those employed in central government, local authorities and in other public bodies such as those industries which were nationalized after the Second World War. Among the employees of central government (civil service) there are, in addition, distinctions between grades and also between categories such as established/non-established, industrial/non-industrial. This may explain some apparent inconsistencies in figures both from primary and secondary sources.

Though there may be some difference between authorities relating to the actual numbers involved, the trend for much of this century has been a steady expansion of public sector employment. Welfare-related occupations have contributed significantly to that process. Between 1902 and 1914 the number of established civil servants working in the social services increased from just over 2000 to 5300. Not surprisingly the largest growth in that period followed the introduction of the National Insurance Scheme in 1911, but there was also a significant increase in the number of civil servants responsible for education and in supervising the activities of local authorities via the Local Government Board (Middleton, 1996a, p. 209). At the outbreak of the Second World War national insurance and pensions accounted for the overwhelming number of civil servants working in the social services sector of central government.

It was, however, the local – rather than central – government labour force which expanded most significantly during the interwar period. Between 1911 and 1938 those working in civil central government increased form 1.5 to 2.6 per cent of the total working population. In local government the increase was from 3.6 to 5.9 per cent between 1911 and 1931, before falling back slightly to 5.6 per cent in 1938

(Middleton, 1996a, p. 345). Education was a major component of that expansion, while the increase in nursing staff consequent on the development of the municipal hospital service after 1929 was estimated at 52 per cent between 1928 and 1938 according to the Society of Medical Officers of Health (Dingwall, Rafferty and Webster, 1988, p. 103).

The sharpest rise in the public sector workforce occurred between 1938 and 1951, and especially after the Second World War. Between those dates Middleton estimates that the number of public sector employees increased from 2.2 million to 6.3 million. As a proportion of the total labour force that represented an increase of from 9.9 to 26.4 per cent. Whilst a sizeable part of that increase can be accounted for by the postwar Labour government's nationalization programme, the expansion of social programmes also contributed to Britain's growing public sector. Health and education are of especial significance. The latter increased steadily from 2.6 per cent of the total workforce in 1951 to 6.4 per cent in 1976, before falling back to 6.0 per cent in 1981. Health showed a continuous rise (after a slow start up to 1961) from 2.1 per cent of the total labour force in 1951 to 4.9 per cent in 1981 (Middleton, 1996a, p. 525). With one million employees, much was made of its position as the largest employer in Western Europe.

Since 1979 there has been a decline in total public employment. This is mainly explained by the privatization programme which the Conservative governments of the 1980s pursued vigorously. In addition there has been a significant reduction in the size of the civil service. Between 1979 and 1995 its numbers fell from 732 000 to just under 517 000 (Rhodes, 1997, p. 89).

The size of the public sector is not the only element which has recently changed: so too has the culture of civil servants and local government officials. Compulsory competitive tendering and the contract culture have reshaped the working practices of local government, while in central government the Next Steps initiative, the process of agencification (*ibid.*) and market testing are all part of the new environment.

From its origins in the NHS in the early 1980s in relation to the 'hotel' services of cleaning, laundry and catering, compulsory competitive tendering (CCT) was introduced into local government services by the Local Government Act of 1988. While there is some unanimity that CCT has 'undoubtedly led to efficiency savings' (Butcher, 1995, p. 112),

Butcher and others have also drawn attention to the 're-ordering of workforce relationships' (Clarke and Newman, 1997, p. 70) which it has brought about. For staff, especially those in working-class occupations in the public sector, it has tended to mean the weakening of trade unions, the decline of collective bargaining and the weakening of equal opportunity issues and procedures. Meanwhile, in terms of service delivery, issues have also been raised about the maintenance of quality standards in a contracted-out service where profit is a predominant concern, as well as the restricted opportunities that exist for the redress of grievance. The introduction of CCT has tended to shift direct service supply further away from the local authorities, to commercial concerns or management buy-outs, for example. That, in turn, suggestively raises questions about why local authorities had such responsibilities in the first place and how effectively those responsibilities were exercised, especially in the period of the classic welfare state.

Meanwhile, in central government the environment of change has involved the creation of semi-autonomous agencies – the Benefits Agency and the Child Support agency are two examples – responsible for operational management, and the introduction of market testing. Under the Next Steps programme initiated in 1988, 70 per cent of the civil service had been organized into agencies by the mid-1990s. Whilst ministers remain responsible and accountable to Parliament for policy, chief executives appointed on a contract basis are responsible for ensuring that the operational objectives of each agency are achieved. Formalizing the division between operational management and policy-making has created 'two civil services: in the policy making core department and in the executive agencies' (Rhodes, 1997, p. 96).

Superimposed upon this division was the introduction in the early 1990s of market testing: 'competition with outside suppliers in order to determine who is best able to provide a particular service on the basis of best long term value for money' (Cm. 1730). This injection of market testing not only overrode 'the freedom of agency chief executives to run their public businesses the way they wished' (Hennessy, 1996, p. 131), it also led one distinguished commentator on constitutional affairs to ponder 'the grand principles of a *grand corps*', the role of the civil service as a profession

> in whatever capacity the public servants are pursuing their calling whether it be as Secretary of the Cabinet...or the administrative

assistant across the counter from the 'customer' in the Benefits Agency or Employment Service local office. (Hennessy, 1996, ch. 5 *passim*)

Such grand thinking, it has been suggested (Harrison, 1996, p. 379), needs also to address the deficits of the system which Next Steps set out to replace – the vagueness of ministerial control and the lack of incentives for staff to restrain the costs of activities over which they had little direct control. The system that has replaced it, however, has also generated criticism, not least about the division between policy and management. This was well-illustrated in the controversy between the then Home Secretary Michael Howard and Derek Lewis the Director General of the Prison Service Agency. But there are also other examples from various parts of the welfare sector where 'government has consistently attempted to distance itself from crises and controversies by insisting that these are not questions of policy or the responsibility of Ministers' (Clarke and Newman, 1997, p. 144). That has led to a second criticism – that of democratic deficit, a term used to identify the declining control of public services by elected representatives. A whole range of intermediate agencies now exist in welfare and related sectors governed by a 'new magistracy' (Stewart, 1993) and managed on more competitive and businesslike principles. This change, however, also raises questions about the representative nature of the 'classic' welfare state as much as it highlights the issues of accountability and redress of grievance in the new public management.

Women and Employment

It is frequently affirmed that the most revolutionary change in the twentieth-century labour force has been the increased participation of women in paid employment. At the beginning of the century over 95 per cent of men aged 15 to 65 claimed an occupation in the census. By contrast, in 1901 only one-third of women aged between 15 and 64 were classified as in paid employment, a figure which remained remarkably constant for the first half of the century. More recently the level of male participation has shown a decline, partly because of a deferred age of entry and a tendency to early retirement. Women's participation rates, by contrast, have increased substantially. In 1951 36 per cent of women aged 20 to 64 were in the labour force. By 1981 that figure had risen to 61 per cent. However a number of historians have argued that it is unwise to regard the post-Second World War increase of women in the labour force as an historic rise. Their argument rests on two foundations: the inadequacy of the statistics for earlier periods, and the likelihood that they underestimated women's paid employment earlier in the century, especially that of part-time work.

What has certainly changed is the pattern of working women's lives. At the beginning of the century more than three-quarters of women aged 15 to 34 were recorded as in paid employment. Beyond that age the figures dropped dramatically: to 13 per cent of those aged between 35 and 44, and to 11 per cent aged 45 to 59 (Thane, 1994, p. 97). Though there were regional and occupational variations, 'in general it may be said that female participation diminished sharply with age and with marriage' (Glynn and Booth, 1996, p. 45). Since the early 1950s it is the increase in the number of married women in the labour force which has been especially striking, rising from 26 per cent of all married women in 1951 to 62 per cent in 1981 (Lewis, 1992a, p. 65). Many factors have been used to explain the growing propensity of married women to enter paid employment. These include smaller families and the shorter period spent in child-bearing and child-rearing; the improvement in – and availability of – labour-saving domestic appliances; the impact of wartime work especially during the Second World War which, it has been suggested (Howlett, 1994, p. 288) seemed 'to change many women's views towards the labour market, particularly younger women who had gained a considerable amount of economic freedom by working for high wages in the munitions factories'.

It needs also to be remembered that the postwar period was one of full employment with an excess of vacancies over unemployed workers. As early as the immediate postwar years it was officially recognized that the prospective labour force fell substantially short of what was required to meet national production objectives. The consequence was a conflict between the Ministry of Labour encouraging women to return to work and the Ministries of Health and Education who were more committed to a traditional view of full-time motherhood (Lewis, 1992a, p. 71). But in explaining the change, as Lewis notes (*ibid.*, p. 67), 'ideas as to what it is appropriate for women to do and as to what women are capable of doing' need also to be taken into account.

The significance of the change can best be appreciated by comparing the postwar period with the years between the wars. As Thane (1994, p. 395) notes, at that time middle-class women entered the labour market for the years between education and marriage and then left it permanently. In a number of occupations such as teaching they were required to do so by the operation of a marriage bar, which excluded married women from paid employment. This has been depicted (Lewis, 1992, p. 68) as the product of gender ideology which benefited men both as workers (by excluding female competition) and as husbands (in securing the unpaid services of full-time housewives). But there were examples, as in the case of female civil servants in the 1920s, where women themselves campaigned for a marriage bar in order to protect the jobs of younger and single women (Bourke, 1994, p. 104). Meanwhile 'working class women tended to take paid work after marriage whenever household finances required it' (Thane, 1994, p. 395). Such work was often part-time, of short duration and hence not recorded in the official statistics. The 'two phase', or 'bi-modal', work pattern established from the 1950s, with women returning to paid employment after child-rearing, was thus at considerable variance with previous practice. It was also the reverse of many of the assumptions on which Beveridge planned his postwar scheme of social security.

Not only has there been an increase in the number of married women in the labour force. The expansion of women's employment has overwhelmingly been in part-time jobs. Between 1951 and 1991 the number of women part-timers in the labour force increased from 754 000 to 4.7 million. Many such jobs tend to be in personal service occupations and characterized by low rates of pay and ineligibility for many of the benefits of full-time employment, such as sickness pay and job security.

In addition to these changes, there has also been a shift in the nature of women's employment. At the beginning of the century domestic service was the largest single source of paid employment. Before the outbreak of the Second World War, however, that sector was already in considerable decline as new employment opportunities became available for women, especially in clerical positions and retailing. The number of women in the civil service, for example, increased from 33 000 to 102 000 in the decade between 1911 and 1921. The expanding public sector thus extended the employment opportunities open to women, a trend that was reinforced after the inauguration of the welfare state. By 1961, for example, women made up 47.5 per cent of the workforce in social welfare and related occupations. There are those who regard this as an enhancement of women's citizenship status, since it provided greater opportunities for economic independence. A contrary view asserts that employment in the welfare sector has perpetuated and reinforced a particular stereotype of women's work, transferring it from the unpaid domestic environment to that of paid labour. In addition it is argued that much of women's work in the welfare sector has been predominantly in unskilled, lower paid jobs. As Williams (1989, p. 181) notes

> it is not simply that...in many cases employers use the cleaning, cooking and caring skills that women have developed in their homes and label it as low paid *unskilled* work, but also that so much of this work is *part-time* and therefore low paid.

Occupational segregation has also been a feature of women's professional employment. At the beginning of the century school teaching and nursing were the most popular professional occupations employing women. Social work, from its nineteenth-century origins, has also been perceived principally as women's work. As with nursing, 'recruitment was divided on class and gender lines' (Hugman, 1991, p. 54). 'Respectable' working-class men and women were employed in certain activities as in Poor Law workhouses or police court missions, for example. Middle-class recruitment was largely of women into casework. This inheritance accounted in large measure for the differences in the statutory personal welfare services initiated in the late 1940s. Untrained men predominated in the local authority welfare departments inherited from the Poor Law, while children's departments were largely and increasingly staffed by trained women. In that new milieu 'women had for the first time been given a route to the top in local government and the Home Office' (Glennerster, 1995a, p. 64). On the integration of children's departments with other local authority personal welfare services in 1971, however, women were in a very definite minority in appointments to the newly created post of Director of Social Services. Throughout the period of the classic welfare state, as for much of the twentieth century, many similar instances could be cited: '[T]he statistical disparity between the numbers of women at the lower levels of most professions and at the top, left discrimination, often unconscious, as the only explanation' (Thane, 1991b, p. 207).

The issue of seniority has been one aspect of discriminatory employment practice. Another has concerned equal pay. The Royal Commission on Equal Pay which reported in 1946 found in the public sector that differentials averaged 50 per cent among lower grades, while the pay of the few women in senior positions was about 10 per cent below that of their male equivalents. The Commission put forward a strong case for equal pay for comparable work but concluded that implementation in the near future would be harmful to the economy. Pressure from trade unionists and women on the issue increased in the early 1950s, and in 1955 the government announced the phased introduction of equal pay into the civil service, local government and teaching.

Thus far the issue of women in employment has been presented as a contrast between women and men. A more recent contrast is that between middle-class professional women working full-time and their lower paid, part-time sisters. Such a divide is not new: but it has become more obvious as salary levels for top professionals have increased and tax rates for those on high earnings have fallen. The implications of this polarization are indicated by Mayo and Weir (1993, p. 44). Women in the professional service class 'are more likely to be able to afford full time child care, which in turn enables them to avoid career breaks and part time work, both of which have been associated with disadvantages and costs for women'. By contrast,

> women in routine clerical and unskilled manual work, the most typical occupations for women, are precisely those who are most likely to become trapped in part time and often casualised part-time work to fit in with their caring responsibilities and most likely to be adversely affected by reductions in public services, such as local authority nurseries and holiday play schemes.

There is much continuity in the interface between women, work and welfare. Though women's position in paid employment has expanded and changed, to a large extent at the end of the century the issues remain those of gender and class, of occupational remuneration and family responsibility.

Professionals and Consumers

During the twentieth century there has been a massive expansion in the number and influence of professionals. For at least one historian (Perkin, 1989) 'the rise of professional society' represents the defining characteristic of the past century. Much of that expansion has taken place in welfare-related occupations in the public sector – medicine, teaching, nursing and social work, for example; and has generated an aura of expertise and bureaucratic paternalism, trenchantly summed up in Barbara Wooton's (1959) phrase 'Daddy knows best'.

The characteristics of a profession have been the subject of extensive sociological discussion. From this literature, four are especially pertinent to this discussion. Of these, the first is specialist education and training which provides the knowledge base for professional practice. To the extent that such professional education is provided within the higher education system, it has been one of the factors explaining the unprecedently large number of students in higher education and the increasingly vocational role for the universities that has occurred in recent decades.

Secondly is the process known as occupational closure. While education and training are important facets of the professional identity, they are not by themselves sufficient to explain the phenomenon of professional power. That is the result also of the social process of occupational closure. By limiting the number of entrants or those accredited, a scarcity value is created for particular skills which in turn enhances professional status. Witz (1992) has argued with regard to the medical profession that exclusionary strategies by men successfully prevented most women from becoming doctors in the nineteenth century and for part of the twentieth century, and kept them in subordinate positions when they were admitted. She has similarly argued that nursing and midwifery, two medical occupations in which women were predominant, have been prevented from gaining full professional recognition by the dominant medical profession.

The third feature of professional work in the twentieth century is that it is increasingly undertaken in bureaucratic organizations. The status of the independent contractor dependent on individual clients for their income has increasingly been replaced by the professional as a salaried employee. Wilding (1982, p. 67) notes that bureaucracies can free professionals from many of the constraints and inhibitions of private practice, but much of the literature focuses on the constraints which it imposes upon professionalism: professionals' subordination to managerial authority and control within the bureaucracy, for example, and the routinisation of much professional work (Cousins, 1987, p. 96).

It is the relationship between the state and the professions that constitutes the fourth defining characteristic of twentieth-century professional activity. In many respects this is a symbiotic relationship which is well-illustrated by the services of the welfare state. On the one hand the state needs professionals to implement its welfare policies, to provide services and to discriminate between those who are eligible and those who are not. On the other hand, it is the state which legitimates particular types of education and training and professional accreditation and which provides a legitimacy to practice.

The privileges which the professions claim

> can only be granted and enforced by government... On the other hand, government needs the professions both... to implement the policies to which it is pledged, and also to advise it on how particular aims might be achieved and how services might best be organised. (Wilding, 1982, p. 67)

This symbiotic relationship is best exemplified in the often-discussed example of the medical profession. The Medical Act, 1858 created the single medical register of approved practitioners and established the General Medical Council to oversee the related activities of education and licensing:

> The significance of the Register, of course, lay in those it excluded. For all ranks of regular practitioners now appeared as 'insiders' lined up against all 'outsiders' – the unqualified homeopaths, medical botanists, quacks, bone-setters and the like who are automatically constituted by exclusion into the 'fringe'. (Porter, 1987, p. 51)

This legal arrangement not only created a sense of legitimate medical practice by distinguishing it from alternative therapies, it also provided the medical profession with a powerful position which it has used successfully and successively in the twentieth-century debate on health care: in the response to the introduction of the Health Insurance Scheme (1911–13) and in its repeated unwillingness to accept local authority control. Yet, paradoxically, during the course of the century the medical profession has come to advocate what it previously resisted. Thus in its *General Medical Service for the Nation* (1938) the British Medical Association (BMA) advocated the extension to the wage-earner's family of the health insurance scheme it had resisted in the early 1910s; just as in the second half of the 1980s the BMA which had been

> the virulent opponent of Aneurin Bevan in 1946 was... most forceful in defending the health service, in denouncing the government for

threatening its existence and failing to fund it as was properly required (Morgan, 1990, p. 494).

It was, of course, in the 1940s creation of the NHS that the power of the medical profession was most clearly evident. As introduced on the Appointed Day – 5 July 1948 – the NHS was the result of negotiation between the government and the medical profession, with the latter achieving significant concessions at the expense of the intentions and aspirations of the former. As Minister of Health, Bevan's task was to organize a National Health Service out of the variegated medical and public health services which already existed. While the service was made comprehensive, universal and free at the point of demand, the actual administrative arrangements (with the tripartite distinction between hospitals, general practitioner services and community health provisions) reflected the separate strands in medical education and training as it had developed since the mid-nineteenth century. Consultants, with their longer and more specialist training and higher status, thus continued to be separated in the new administrative arrangements from the shorter and less specialized training of general practitioners who themselves were to be distinct from those whose training prepared them to deal with issues of environmental health in the nineteenth-century public health tradition. In that way, the existing divisions and structures of British medicine formed the basis for the new administrative arrangements of the NHS in the 1940s. They both created – and reinforced – a power relationship within the profession with the hospital-based consultants at its apex.

Bevan not only had to organize a National Health Service from the inheritance of past experience. He also had to ensure that it was staffed. That was the political and professional issue which dominated the period between the passage of the NHS Act in 1946 up to the day appointed for its implementation. The crucial issue was the opposition of GPs to a variety of factors – real and imagined – involved in working in the new service, especially what they perceived as the threat of salaried employment. Within weeks of the Act a poll of GPs had registered a 64 per cent vote against participating in the new service, and as late as April 1948 there were still 10 000 opposed to the new service compared with the maximum total of 17 000 recorded earlier. It was not until the end of May 1948 – just over a month away from the Appointed Day – that the GPs agreed to join the NHS. That they did so owed much to the way in which Bevan used the divisions within the medical establishment. The consultants 'were offered many fresh inducements without being expected to sacrifice too many of their traditional privileges' (Webster, 1988a, p. 305) in order to secure the compliance of the humbler general practitioners:

> In 1912 Lloyd George had aimed to by-pass the elite to get at the humble working doctor; Bevan used the elite to capture the GP. In effect he bought off ('stuffed their mouths with gold' were his words) the consultants and used them as a counter-weight to break down the resistance of the BMA. (Fraser, 1984, p. 235)

The NHS may have offered a new deal in health care to the British people, but its creation represented an accommodation between politicians and professionals which strengthened the old medical division between generalists and specialists.

Welfare professionals have not only exercised their power in the policy-making arena and in the administrative shape of welfare services. In addition, their power to define needs and problems has implications for the practice of welfare work in at least two respects. The first centres around issues of care and control. The professionals who define needs and problems are the same personnel who also 'define and impose criteria of "normality", "deviance" or personal "adequacy" which, as many critics have pointed out, stigmatise and make dependent welfare clients' (Cousins, 1987, p. 94). Welfare professionals thus face Janus-like in the two directions of care and control: though Hugman (1991, p. 120) notes there are certain welfare professions such as probation work and social work with juvenile offenders where 'the use of social-work-trained staff enables social control to work through the guise of social care'.

The second implication centres on issues of inter-agency working. A variety of such initiatives have been developed over the past twenty years – joint planning, joint finance and partnership programmes – which have been advocated on the grounds of economy, efficiency and effectiveness. Yet academic studies and official inquiries have repeatedly indicated professional and organizational resistance to closer collaboration. This is because it is perceived as a threat both to organizational boundaries and empires and a challenge to the definition of needs and problems according to specific expertise and training. At service delivery level especially, both these factors have worked against the lofty aspirations of the policy of community care.

Professional power holding has not been without its critics. One of the most trenchant was Illich's (1977) critique of 'the disabling professions' which he accused of creating a dependence on professional intervention and thereby removing the individual's capacity for independent, self-reliant action. 'While initially people became dependent on the professionals for specialist skills, gradually they became dependent on them for services which, in the past, people provided for themselves or each other'. Much of the Illich-inspired critique of professions has centred on medical care. Perkin (1989, p. 348) for example observes that 'a health service defined and dominated by treatment specialists was bound to be a sickness-oriented system rather than a programme for public health', while other studies have looked, for example, at the medicalization of women's experience in child-birth, conception and menstruation.

Illich, however, is only one of a considerable number who over the past 30 years have been critical of the exercise and implications of professional power. In Britain that critique began on the political left. In a lecture delivered in 1951 Richard Titmuss (1963, p. 27) was concerned that 'as the social services become more complex, more specialised and subject to a finer division of labour they become less intelligible to the lay councillor or public representative'. The question, as he saw it in the immediate aftermath of the creation of the classic welfare state, was whether welfare professionals were 'prepared to assume greater social responsibilities to match their added knowledge and the power that accompanies it'. It was an issue which, as he subsequently argued in *The Irresponsible Society* (1963, p. 216), also involved those in the private (especially insurance) sector who, he believed, 'would increasingly become the arbiters of welfare and amenity for larger sections of the community'. A variant of this critique highlighted the intrusive power of professional surveillance within the everyday life of individual citizens, and the personal experience which many users of the welfare state had of their encounters with its professionals and bureaucrats:

> Whether in the growing dole queues or in the waiting rooms of an overburdened NHS or suffering the indignities of Social Security, the corporatist state is increasingly experienced by them not as a beneficence but as a powerful bureaucratic imposition on the people. (Hall 1985, p. 108)

This type of experience became part of the developing critique of the welfare state in the 1980s. Part of that built upon what Perkin (1989,

p. 390) termed 'the condescension of professionalism'. 'This indeed was the Achilles' heel of professionalism through which entered the spears of individual arrogance, collective condescension towards the laity, and mutual disdain between the professions'. But the 1980s critique was a composite of a diversity of factors that coalesced around the political challenge to public sector welfare in general and the growth of government spending in proportion to the economy. Professionals, especially those in the public sector, were inevitably in the eye of the Thatcherite storm. 'However, finely honed their skills and however much their expertise was valued, Thatcher felt that they were insufficiently responsive to market forces – and thus a collective impediment to the achievement of the kind of world she wished to bring about' (Evans, 1997, p. 65). In essence, it represented a clash of world views between a traditional and consensual public service ethos that was perceived to be a self-interested defender of the *status quo* and the vision of a new, thrusting, entrepreneurial and competitive society that would offer greater choice, enhance individual freedom and break down the bureau-professional control of monopoly services. ' "Arrogant" professionals were arraigned alongside "inflexible" bureaucrats and "interfering" politicians as preventing efficient, effective and economic public services' (Clarke *et al.*, 1994, p. 23). By the early 1990s the new world for welfare professionals was one in which a system of general management had been introduced into the NHS, opt-outs provided for schools and hospitals from direct local – or health – authority control, competitive internal markets created which separated the functions of purchasers and providers, with greater opportunities for the newly designated welfare 'consumers' (or at least some of them) to exercise 'exit' and 'voice'. 'If "markets" and "customers" have been the ideological cutting edge of these changes, then "management" has been the eagerly sought principle of articulation for a new organisational regime for the welfare state' (Clarke *et al.*, 1994, p. 25).

At least in theory, and to some degree in practice, professional autonomy is more constrained than previously both by the new public management and a developing consumerism. Though some similarities exist between these challenges to professional dominance, the role of the consumer remains ambiguous in the evolving system of late twentieth-century welfare. While more services have introduced measures of consumer care and satisfaction, there is still little evidence to suggest that service-users are becoming more actively involved in decision-making processes, although experimental 'citizen juries' have recently discussed issues of prioritizing – or rationing – the supply of health care in particular localities.

The consumer interest in welfare may have been shaped by its subordinate position in the welfare state for much of this century. More recent strategies designed to increase user-empowerment have highlighted the tension between choice and control and individual and collective interests in the welfare state. For Alcock (1996, p. 279) choice and control represent divergent means to achieve increased consumer empowerment. As we have already noted, the extension of consumer choice was one of the principal features of welfare reform advocated by the Conservative New Right in the 1980s. Choice was to be extended both by stimulating an increase in the number of suppliers outside the state (which was invariably achieved by means of state subsidy) and by introducing greater competition into public services. One of the lessons of the historical experience, however, is that the 'pure' market operates in favour of those already advantaged and offers no guarantee against monopoly provision. Meanwhile quasi-markets such as were introduced into health, education and social care do not create sufficient conditions for consumer sovereignty since they often leave the choice in the hands of surrogate consumers or professionals.

The alternative model – that of control – highlights the tension between individual and collective interests in the welfare state. At one level, control suggests that individuals have the right and opportunity to seek redress of grievances arising from decisions that affect them. A number of mechanisms exist with this objective, but tribunals first introduced in the National Insurance legislation of 1911 are probably the longest established. They have served as a model for other welfare state services such as health and education. Other and more recent examples include the Parliamentary Commissioner for Administration (the Ombudsman), the Health Service Commissioner and a number of local Commissioners for Administration. Several writers, however, have pointed out that redress of grievance or maladministration can only effectively be assessed in the context of a 'framework of rights, standards of performance and legitimate expectations' (Deakin and Wright, 1990, p. 213). That is the significance of the 'charter' movement initiated by John Major in the early 1990s, though such standard-setting statements originated with a number of local authorities. The first annual report of the Citizen's Charter (Cm. 2101, 1992, p. 1) pointed out:

Through these charters the citizen can increasingly put pressure upon those responsible for providing services to deliver them to a high standard, rather as commercial competition puts consumer pressure on the performance of private sector organisations.

Each of these strategies, however, focuses upon the individual and is largely reactive.

A stronger version of control affirms the importance of involving users more actively in the processes of policy and delivery. User-participation became part of the welfare state agenda from the late 1960s (Richardson, 1983). For all sorts of reasons, not least the civil rights movement in the USA, it was a time when 'the very things which had once commended state planning to those who advocated it – bureaucracy and professionalism – were seen to be making government remote from the people whom it was intended to serve' (Finlayson, 1994, p. 305). From the early 1970s a whole variety of schemes were introduced designed to create the image of a more participatory welfare state. These included the creation of Community Health Councils as part of the 1974 reorganization of the NHS, the addition of parents to school governing bodies, and consultation with tenants likely to be affected by a matter of housing management. User-involvement was also a feature of the community care reforms introduced in the early 1990s. In each of these sectors, however, there has been concern about the representativeness of those involved and the method of their selection, as well as whether in practice such attempts to give the users a 'voice' has shifted the balance of power away from professionals and managers in the direction of more user-friendly and flexible services.

Beresford (1997) has suggested that the relationship between producers and consumers remains social policy's 'last social division'. For him the way forward to a 'truly egalitarian and socially constructed social policy' (ibid., p. 218) lies in a recognition of the contribution made by organizations of disabled people and survivors of psychiatric care over the past few years. Such movements have developed their own research and knowledge, methods of self-organization and user-led alternatives to conventional service provision. Insofar as other groups of welfare users can develop such approaches, he believes it holds out the prospect of a more flexible, postmodern welfare system in which those who use the services are recognized to have their own expertise about the sort of services they require. Such a vision of a user-led welfare system would not only entail a new relationship between professional and consumer. It would also turn on its head many of the assumptions about professional and managerial control that have dominated the welfare state's development during the twentieth century.

7

GENDER, CLASS AND GENERATION

Social justice is concerned with who ought to get what.

(P. Taylor-Gooby, 1997)

Despite growth in national wealth, age old inequalities remain.

(Frank Field, 1973)

Previous chapters have indicated some of the divisions and differences that exist within the welfare state: between the politicians and those who are most affected by their decisions, taxpayers and service users, professionals, managers and consumers. All of this calls into question the view of the welfare state as universalist and solidaristic. That view has also been challenged by analyses based upon gender, class and generation. There is a strong interrelationship between these three facets of what can be considered a modern social division of welfare. Central to each of them, for example, are the concepts of access, distribution and output, and common to them all is the idea that people of different social class, sex and age experience welfare in different ways. In part this is the consequence of the social construction of dependency of particular parts of the life-cycle, such as childhood and old age. It also has to do with how welfare is delivered and the assumptive worlds which govern both policy and practice as, for example, in the insurance basis of social security provision and the gendered assumptions about caring responsibilities. But it also raises issues that surround the complex interrelationship of work and welfare, not only in the sense of jobs that provide extensive occupational benefits, but also of the ways in which an individual's employment experience may affect their 'life chances' during

133

working life and condition the choices that are available to them in old age.

In its discussion of the often interrelated themes of gender, class and generation, this chapter aims to provide an analysis of the twentieth-century welfare state in terms of 'the continuing contest over the structure, character and distribution of power and resources in the modern world' (Harris, 1991, p. 58).

Gender

The gender perspective is a comparatively recent innovation in the analysis of welfare, and of the welfare state in particular. It played no part, for example, in Richard Titmuss's seminal discussion of the social division of welfare of the late 1950s. Its origin is usually traced to Elizabeth Wilson's *Women and the Welfare State* published in 1977, a book 'written particularly for the women (and men) who work for the welfare state, and for the women, housewives, mothers and workers who are subject to its sexist ideology. It is intended as an exposure of that ideology. It is also a call to fight it' (Wilson, 1977, pp. 41–2). Since that time the feminist perspective has become increasingly sophisticated and diverse. Most contemporary studies tend to distinguish between liberal, socialist, radical and Black feminism (Williams, 1989). While such differences have produced different strategies for challenging male domination in social policy, in general 'feminists have made the issues of who controls welfare and how it is organised, questions of immediate concern and political priority' (Williams, 1989, p. 86). Studies within this paradigm have thus documented 'the inequalities between women and men as recipients of welfare state services' as well as emphasising 'a different set of determinants shaping the nature of public policy provision of welfare' (Sainsbury, 1994, p. 2). The result has been that over the past 20 years feminist scholarship has challenged 'the universalist rhetoric employed by policy-makers and many earlier scholars [by] pointing out that the ostensible "universal" welfare states are often deeply structured along gender lines' (Stevenson, 1995, p. 382).

The literature on women and the welfare state is extensive. Within the genre, however, it is possible to identify three principal and often interrelated themes: women as producers, as consumers and as agents in the development of welfare states.

The role of women as welfare providers both in paid employment and in the 'private' domain of the family owes much to recent feminist research and is in sharp contrast to 'the gender-blind nature of earlier studies of the welfare state' which portrayed 'women ... not in the role of producers but as consumers of welfare' (Digby and Stewart, 1996, p. 18). Recent research by contrast has highlighted women's role in the production of welfare that developed during the nineteenth century: in nursing and teaching, in local government, as elected guardians, and as lady visitors in workhouses and infirmaries, in addition to their extensive work in philanthropy. In the twentieth century, as the previous chapter noted, health, education and welfare-related occupations have become a significant locus of women's paid employment. Such trends, it has been argued, have promoted and reinforced occupational segregation while at the same time consigning many women to low paid, low status employment as welfare producers.

The segregation between men's work and women's work can be seen in the gender division of labour that characterized many of the nineteenth-century philanthropic organizations. Men were concerned with finance and committee business, while women undertook the role of organizer and engaged in personal service work. A recent survey of voluntary activity (Lynn and Davis Smith, 1991) suggests a similar predisposition for men to be involved with committee work. In addition, it also shows a gender bias in the kind of voluntary work in which men and women engage (Sheard, 1995, p. 120). Men are more likely to be involved with sports, hobbies, advice work and transport, women with health and social welfare, church and school-related activities and fund raising. Many social programmes initiated by voluntary activity in the nineteenth century became incorporated into the state during the twentieth century. The work of visiting mothers and children, for example, became health visiting carried out by local authority staff. In the process it has been argued that

> to a large extent the growth of welfare provision has often reinforced occupational segregation through the creation of jobs that have been occupied almost exclusively by women, such as nurses, primary school teachers or social workers. (Alcock, 1996, p. 226)

Meanwhile it has also been argued that many women's experience as producers of welfare in the paid sector is of low-status, low-paid work: an experience reinforced by a variety of recent trends. For Hugman

(1991, p. 177) the development of aides, auxiliaries and assistants in the caring professions has drawn women into 'their lower echelons'. At the same time, however, they have been excluded 'from hierarchical advancement through the creation and maintenance of boundaries to qualified practitioner and management grades'. Millar (1997, p. 106) meanwhile has assessed the impact of privatization programmes on women's employment in the welfare state. Not only have they meant 'job losses for many women who were working in the public sector'. In addition, 'those who have been transferred to the private cleaning and catering companies have seen their pay and conditions deteriorate'.

Women not only provide welfare in the arena of paid employment. They are also the principal providers of unpaid, 'tending' care for children, adults with dependencies and older people. This has also been one of the important dimensions of welfare supply which has been opened up by the feminist perspective, not least in relation to what is euphemistically termed 'community care'. How and why women care has been the subject of extensive investigation and discussion; but the way in which the 'costs' of care fall disproportionately upon women has highlighted the ambivalent relationship between the state and the family and raised questions of equal opportunities between men and women. Land and Rose (1985, p. 93) symbolize the former in their argument that 'for women to be free not to give as well as to give requires that there are good alternative services'; while Finch and Groves (1980, p. 511) expose the tension between community care and equal opportunities:

> The onus is on any government which leaves equal opportunities legislation on the statute book to demonstrate that the promotion of equal opportunities is a commitment which pervades all its practices including those relating to community care. Without that intention equal opportunities legislation represents nothing more than pious hypocrisy.

Women also consume welfare. According to a recent study (Hills, 1993), on average women are net lifetime beneficiaries of the welfare state, while men are net lifetime payers. This is perhaps not altogether surprising since women have a longer life expectancy than men and also – significantly – have shorter periods in paid employment. Furthermore, in general men have higher earnings and pay more tax than women. When such general trends are disaggregated, however, a more diverse picture begins to emerge.

First, women may benefit from some sectors of the welfare state more than others. As Thane (1996, p. 284) notes:

> if women have made fewer gains from a welfare state than women hoped at the beginning of the century... women gained immensely from the introduction of the NHS and from an education system from which by the 1990s females were gaining more than males in terms of examination success.

Secondly in considering welfare consumers the contrast, as the last chapter observed, is not only between women and men but also between women themselves. Mayo and Weir (1993, pp. 51–2), for example, note the contrast between ' "service" class professional/managerial women in two-earner households on the one hand and women caught up in the poverty trap, in unemployed households or as single parents on the other'. Thirdly, research on women's continuing financial vulnerability within the welfare state suggests that it is the consequence of the inter-relationship of a variety of factors. These include social and demo-graphic changes, women's position in the paid labour market and the assumptive worlds which continue to underpin the social security system.

Lewis and Piauchaud's (1992, p. 43) review of women and poverty in the twentieth century indicates that towards the end of the century 'women constitute a roughly similar proportion of the poor today as in 1900'. Over the century, however, the composition of female poverty has altered significantly. Whereas in the early twentieth century 'married women were the largest group in poverty because of low wages paid to husbands and because of large families... today female poverty is concentrated among lone women'. 'Lone women' itself is a shorthand expression which covers a variety of female experience: but within this category those who have the highest risk and the longest duration of poverty are older women living alone – whose circumstances will be discussed more fully in the section of the chapter concerned with generation – and lone mothers (Millar, 1997, p. 99).

While there are a number of routes into lone motherhood – divorce, separation, widowhood or extra marital conception – their experience is united by the absence of shared income from a spouse for extended periods (Evandrou and Falkingham, 1995, p. 175). There are, however, similarities and differences within this experience. Single lone mothers and widowed lone mothers, for example, both experience particularly low earnings as a result of their lower labour force activity. But in terms of social security benefits there is a considerable difference between them; widows are treated more favourably than other categories of single motherhood. For some this reflects a continuation of the moral distinction between deserving and undeservingness. For others it highlights the ambiguity between theory and practice within the welfare state. While in theory modern welfare states may have tended towards the view that 'women's primary duty is motherhood', in practice 'their access to social welfare programmes has been, as per Beveridge's proposals, determined by marriage rather than motherhood' (Lewis, 1992a, p. 33).

Beveridge himself favoured the introduction of a separation benefit (Cmd. 6404, paras 311, 347) as a means of replacement income in cases of marital breakdown. But his proposal foundered over the issue of fault. As a result, lone mothers – with the exception of widows – were excluded from the National Insurance scheme and had to rely on assistance-based benefits. Jane Millar (1994, p. 70) outlines the steady increase in the number and proportion of lone parents (mainly women) receiving social assistance payments over the previous half century. That growth was especially pronounced after 1971 which she attributes especially to the decline in employment rates for lone mothers (though lone fathers also appear to have suffered the same fate). 'As employment fell, receipt of benefits increased rapidly and . . . poverty increased'. There were also those who argued contrariwise that state support for lone mothers had gone too far, creating a perverse incentive in favour of lone parenthood and against marriage (see for example Morgan, 1995). It was from this set of circumstances that the Child Support Agency (CSA) was established in the early 1990s. It was created ostensibly to ensure an effective level of child support, transfer responsibility from publicly financed assistance to absent fathers, and symbolically to underscore the mutual responsibilities which family members owe to each other. Since its creation, the CSA has been the subject of considerable criticism. A recent national client survey (Hutton *et al.*, 1998) indicated that while absent parents tended to agree with the Agency's aims, they were critical of many facets of its practical operation.

Beveridge regarded divorce as an exceptional circumstance, a fact which made his discussion historically contingent. But it has also been observed that Beveridge's social security proposals were based upon a gendered division of labour, with the man earning what was construed as a 'family' wage while his wife provided domestic work in the home. Thus a scheme of contributory insurance such as Beveridge proposed offered protection to the male against unemployment whilst the married women's protection rested on the rights she acquired through her husband on marriage. Recent historical research has produced a more sophisticated analysis, though it retains a gendered perspective. It has been noted how Beveridge wrestled with the issue of women's entitlement and spent considerable time trying to incorporate especially married women into his system. His solution was to treat housewives 'not as dependants of their husbands but as partners' (Cmd. 6404, para. 117).

As successive writers have noted, however, it was partnership in which 'the parties were to be equal but different' (Lewis, 1996, p. 220). It was based on separate spheres of work for men and women and the legally enforceable rights which the married woman had to maintenance from her husband. For this reason, therefore, 'the state had no duty or right to supplant the economic relationship between man and wife, only to supplement them when it came to provision for children' (Glennerster and Evans, 1994, p. 64). But it has also been observed that Beveridge's view on women's role in the partnership was the product of the tension between two essentially incompatible ideals: 'the ideal of the economically independent citizen and the ideal of the indispensable mother in the home' (Harris, 1994, p. 34). The end result of this tension was that 'married women were accordingly invited to take the "married women's option" paying less by way of contributions and collecting less in benefits' (Lewis, 1996, p. 220).

For Pedersen (1993, p. 340) and for many other writers such a result denied women full citizenship within the welfare state:

> The Beveridge Plan claimed to be a blue-print for a welfare state with 'separate but equal' provisions for men and women. Yet the fundamental imbalance remained: a married women's entitlements, being based on the assumption that her work was unremunerated, could scarcely be equal to her husband's.

What, then, of women's agency in the development of the welfare state? This cannot be separated from the issue of women's enfranchisement though it cannot be entirely explained by it either. All women over 30 acquired the right to vote in general elections in 1918; in 1928 the age was equalized at 21 for men and women.

We have already noted recent research which has suggested that women played a distinctive role in the plethora of charitable enterprises that characterized Victorian England. They combined 'a growing expertise in management [with] a continuing personal involvement with the clients' (Digby and Stewart, 1996, p. 9). That dual contribution has been discussed in a variety of recent studies (see, for example, Lewis, 1991, 1995). Localism was the essence of such work. As Digby and Stewart (1996, p. 10) note:

> Victorian women's social work in housing, poor law, health or education was performed locally, cementing links between family and community and acting as a bridge from activist women's own families to the families of the poor whom they aimed to regenerate morally.

It was women, Lord Salisbury pointed out in 1899 'who are in closer touch with [the poor] than any man can be. What touch there is, what contact there is, between the working classes and the classes that are above them...passes almost entirely through the hands of women' (cited in Hollis, 1987, p. 20).

In addition to their work in voluntary organizations, in the later nineteenth and early twentieth centuries women also became involved in the statutory services of the local state: as members of School Boards from 1870, as Poor Law guardians after 1875 and then by serving as local councillors where they tended to specialize in welfare areas such as health, housing, the Poor Law and local government. Women thus embodied the symbiotic relationship between the local state and the voluntary sector that has been described as characteristic of late-Victorian and Edwardian England:

> Where local authority work required personal service, befriending, counselling it was usually devolved to voluntary hands and ladies committees; where a voluntary group operating on the fringe of public work was strapped for cash or short of coercive power (as with children at risk) they pressed tasks on to local authorities (*ibid.*, p. 20).

In this way female activity in the local spheres of statutory and voluntary social action enable us to see women not only as clients but as 'shapers of welfare programs and policies' (Koven and Michel, 1989, p. 113).

Many such programmes specifically focused on issues of especial concern to women – housing, child welfare and women's health – and commanded some support from women in all political parties. Raising such issues, however, presented difficulties in each of the political parties. Much is made of 'the aggressively male ambience of the inter-war labour movement dominated as it was by trade unionists' especially in the debate about family allowances; though as Thane (1991a, p. 110) shows, trade union opposition was not unanimous. Pugh (1992, p. 129) has suggested that, compared to Labour women, women in the interwar Conservative Party were on a more equal social class footing with their leaders. Those same leaders – especially Baldwin and Chamberlain – however, also recognized the need to stay in touch with the average woman voter, a stance which led them to marginalize the more reactionary views from the Conservative Women's Association. While Conservative women in general showed themselves 'very unsympathetic to social reforms' (*ibid*, p. 129), during the 1930s especially there was a considerable coalescence between the progressive presentation of women's issues and Labour's evolving programme in the aftermath of its political defeat in 1931 (Brooke, 1992). 'Together with the emphasis on health and welfare reforms this gave Labour extra credibility amongst women during the war years and brought dividends in the era of the welfare state' (Pugh, 1992, p. 138).

But that welfare state even further eroded the tradition of localism and made welfare issues the province of the central state. For women's agency this had two principal consequences. While women in the earlier twentieth century had made the transition from voluntary visitor to paid employee, they very rarely moved to paid policy-making positions in the civil service. As Lewis (1994, p. 50) notes, 'while British male settlers like William Beveridge moved into policy making positions as the balance of the mixed economy of welfare shifted in favour of the state, women did not'. But furthermore 'the importance attached to the personal service work that was [women's] special provision diminished with the concomitant shift in the philosophy of social provision'. The agenda of universalism was one that encompassed the interests both of women and men.

Class[1]

'Class differences remain at the centre of any understanding of the operation of social policy in Britain' (Alcock, 1996, p. 225). Such an assessment both calls into question the egalitarian objectives of the 'classic' welfare state and highlights the more complex interrelationship that exists between the welfare state and capitalist society. Welfare theorists have characterized this relationship in two alternative ways (Esping-Andersen, 1990, p. 55). Neo-Marxists suggest that the welfare state reproduces the inequalities of the existing class society. In their model 'welfare policies provide the legitimacy and social calm required by monopoly capitalism'. The alternative social democratic perspective regards welfare reform as 'a major contribution to the declining salience of class': welfare 'eliminates the essential causes of class struggle [and] incorporates the working classes'.

The latter view is especially associated with T. H. Marshall (1950) whose analysis delivered in lectures at Cambridge at the end of the 1940s remains an important point of departure for any assessment of the relationship between the welfare state and the system of social stratification. For Marshall the creation of the welfare state in the 1940s was the latest stage in Britain's evolving history of expanding citizenship. Progressively through the eighteenth to the twentieth centuries, he argued, British citizenship was extended, first of all, to incorporate legal rights – equality before the law; then political rights, achieved by means of the extension of the franchise and the introduction of the secret ballot; and finally social rights specifically as the result of the welfare state legislation. In Marshall's analysis such social rights promote 'an equality of status helping counterweigh disparities of income and class (Baldwin, 1990, p. 4):

> Marshall's formulation caught the aspirations embodied in the welfare [state] better than any other. The rich man and the poor man would collect the same pensions from the post office counter, and sit next to each other in the same doctor's waiting room. They would be no less rich or poor for doing so, but they would be much more citizens of one community. (Marquand, 1988a, p. 29)

---

[1] At this point I draw on material from an earlier essay 'The welfare state and the state of welfare' in Gladstone (ed.) (1995).

Entitlement would thus create an equality of status which, in its turn, would be the means of securing social cohesion, integration and solidarity. In these terms, the welfare state was the fulfilment of fraternity, the creation of community.

But in those terms it had its immediate critics. Some on the political right saw the welfare state as a threat to the existing system of social differentiation, especially to the position of the middle class, and as a harbinger of a totalitarian state regime:

> Education, other than that provided in state-aided schools becomes more and more costly, while some politicians would abolish it altogether. Medical attention is being 'equalised' and those who wish to obtain it outside the NHS must pay twice.... Finally, not only are legacies taxed, but keen socialists broadcast their longing to abolish completely the transmission of wealth in any form. (Lewis and Maude, 1949, p. 221)

Nor was there unanimity on the political Left that what had been accomplished in the welfare state legislation represented the establishment of socialism. This issue was central to the second phase of Labour's postwar period in power. After 1948, there was increasing recognition that Labour needed a new vision. But opinion differed as to what form such a new vision should take. *Tribune* called for 'a socialist philosophy based on a fresh and unprejudiced analysis of the difficulties that confront us', while Michael Young and others, critical of the statist tendencies in the postwar economic and social settlement, sought 'to set socialism in the context of freedom and democracy' (Brooke, 1992, p. 339). Morgan's (1984, p. 503) judicious conclusion at the end of his study of *Labour in Power 1945–1951* is that while the Attlee government 'brought the British labour movement to the zenith of its achievement as a political instrument for humanitarian reform ... it did so by evading, rather than resolving, those dilemmas inherent in the potent, beguiling vision of socialism in our time'.

More recent assessments are somewhat less ambiguous about Labour's postwar period in government. Tomlinson (1997, p. 266), for example, suggests that although Labour had a general theoretical belief in equality, in government its practical politics centred on the notion of insecurity which it considered could best be tackled by the introduction of the universal minimum. This focus on 'minimum universalism' had contradictory effects on equality of outcome:

On the one hand, in so far as everyone was given access to minimum levels of income, education and health care, the gap between the position of the poor and that of higher income groups was reduced. On the other hand, for those who had previously paid for health and education, and found the standard of the new free service acceptable, major benefits accrued from no longer having to pay, and inequality increased.

It was a view expressed more contemporaneously by Brian Abel-Smith. For him, 'the main effect of the post-war development of the social services . . . has been to provide free social services to the middle classes' (1958, p. 57). This is not to deny that universal services have not benefited their working-class consumers. It is, however, to argue that the impact of the welfare state has been less solidaristic and benign than Marshall's interpretation suggested. Hay (1996, p. 73) for example, hypothesizes that rather than progressively abating class inequalities, the impact of the welfare state has been rather to 'progressively abate class consciousness, while in fact legitimating deep seated structures of class inequality'.

Since the 1960s especially there has been much research which has emphasized the persisting influence of social class within the welfare state. Alcock (1996, p. 223) provides a useful summary of major work by Atkinson, Townsend and Halsey:

> Social security may have prevented extreme hardship, but the low level of benefits that it provides still mean that those dependent on them live at standards significantly below those of the majority of the working population. Indeed in relative terms the position of social security claimants has remained more or less constant as a proportion of average wage levels throughout most of the twentieth century in Britain. Despite the success of the NHS in providing free health care for all, class differences in the experience of ill-health (morbidity) and the risk of early death (mortality) also remain. Equality of opportunity in education has not prevented class inequalities being reflected in levels of achievement.

Meanwhile Le Grand (1982) called into question the conventional assumption that public spending on welfare was benefiting the less well-off. Contrary to that view, his research indicated that almost all public expenditure on the social services benefited the better off rather than the poor. His conclusions were stark:

In all the relevant areas there persist substantial inequalities in public expenditure, in use, in opportunity, in access and in outcomes. (p. 7)

Basically the forces which created inequalities in the first place and which perpetuate them seem to be too strong to be resisted through indirect methods such as public expenditure on the social services. (p. 137)

The decade in which Le Grand's study appeared – the 1980s – witnessed a considerable expansion of the 'middle-class welfare state' as well as a growing division between rich and poor in British society. We have already noted in a previous chapter the changes which the Conservative government introduced to taxation. In addition to those changes which benefited especially the highest taxpayers, Pugh (1994, p. 313) notes how the elements of the middle-class welfare state such as mortgage-interest tax relief and the tax incentives for personal pensions were financed 'partly by extra taxes on consumption . . . and by reductions in those parts of the welfare system that benefited the working classes'. Among these he instances especially changes in rules governing unemployment benefits and the changes to the social assistance scheme: restrictions to benefits for young people, the introduction of Income Support, and the Social Fund which offered loans instead of grants as previously.

It is to 1979 and the election of Margaret Thatcher's government that critics look for the beginnings of the strategy of inequality and the crumbling of the postwar consensus. That year 'represented a watershed in British social policy: the replacement of a weak and highly circumscribed consensus on the case for combating poverty – which at least kept the issue on the political agenda, however low down its position – with a proactive strategy of inequality' (Walker, 1997b, p. 5).

That strategy looked to the past – and specifically to the Victorian period – for its inspiration, not least in a reduced role for the state and its vision of entrepreneurial activity stimulated by financial incentives creating a 'trickle down' effect to benefit the rest of society. A variety of official data and independent inquiries published recently has indicated that far from wealth 'trickling down', inequality has increased since the late 1970s whether measured by income, expenditure or wealth. This is usefully summarised in Oppenheim (1997b, pp. 22–5). Meanwhile Hills (1996b, pp. 14–15) reviewing the principal findings of the Rowntree *Inquiry into Income and Wealth* points out that:

the gradual, and uneven, reduction in the inequality of income ended in the late 1970s, and income inequality in the United Kingdom grew rapidly in the 1980s, more than reversing the previous post-war fall. Meanwhile, the inequality of wealth distribution reduced substantially up to the mid-1970s, but has since levelled out.

It is not enough, however, to analyse class only in relation to the public sector of welfare. One of the central themes of Titmuss's (1963, p. 55) seminal essay on the social division of welfare was to challenge the stereotypical image of an all-pervasive welfare state for the working classes. There was, in addition, he pointed out, the welfare produced by occupational schemes (the 'perks' of the job) and the fiscal benefits that accrued through the tax system. For Titmuss these varied welfare systems represented, on the one hand, attempts 'to compensate for the growth of dependency in modern society'. But, on the other, their autonomous and separate provision meant that they were 'simultaneously enlarging and consolidating the area of social inequality'. In that respect they ran counter to the solidaristic cohesion that was implicit in social democratic welfare capitalism.

The position of the private sector has always presented a particular challenge to Labour. The Attlee government is again instructive. McKibbin (1998, pp. 534–5), for example, has recently pointed to the contrast between its abolition of the voluntary hospitals while maintaining the existence of the independent sector – the public schools – in education. Such a decision had more than an immediate effect:

> once a decision had been made to exclude from the Labour government's programme those areas of society which would be strongly defended at the only moment when their defences might have been overcome with popular support, the Labour Party let slip an opportunity which was unlikely ever to recur.

Labour's doomed attempt to return to the public school question when in government in the 1960s would appear to provide sufficient validation for that assessment.

The issue of private welfare, however, concerns not only the past: it is an issue of the present and for the future. Over recent years, private welfare has become a more significant feature of individual packages of welfare, though in some sectors – such as housing, pensions and health insurance – more than in others, where unemployment protection is a good case in point. In policy terms, freedom and choice have become more the *lingua franca* of welfare discussion than concepts such as equality and fairness. While the latter resonate with wartime connotations and the notion of a national minimum, the former are considered more appropriate to a more affluent society in which individuals have become more used to consumer choice in many other aspects of their lives. Yet 'in a society that can employ only perhaps half its population more or less continuously through their lives, occupational and private welfare will be fragile for very many people' (Glennerster, 1992b, p. 13).

That assessment impacts also on the future. Forward-looking strategies increasingly emphasize greater self-provision, individual responsibility and the creation of public–private partnerships. Such developments raise both ideological and organizational questions. Central among them is whether private welfare complements state supply or whether it provides an alternative and differentiated system (Brunsdon, 1997, p. 159). Within the Fabian paradigm, collectively provided services were favoured because of the moral superiority of universalism and the belief that public services 'reserved for the poor' would be poor services. The issue remains one of considerable controversy in the debate about the future shape of Britain's welfare state. In Esping-Andersen's (1990, p. 26) characterization, however, future choice may not be significantly different from that past experience in which Britain and most of the Anglo-Saxon world preserved 'an essentially modest universalism in the state [while allowing] the market to reign for the growing social strata demanding superior welfare'.

Generation

Until recently, generation has received less attention in studies assessing the impact of the welfare state than either gender or class. Recent research, however, has rediscovered Rowntree's concept of the life-cycle. In the considerably changed demographics of the late twentieth century it has been shown to have a continuing importance for the analysis of financial insecurity. But its more recent usage has also highlighted the role played by welfare policies themselves in the socially constructed dependencies of childhood and old age, not least through the increasing demarcation between work and welfare which has been one of the characteristics of the twentieth-century welfare state. As such, therefore, generation needs to be examined along with gender and class in any discussion of the social division of welfare.

The nineteenth century was overwhelmingly a youthful society: the demographic factors of fertility and mortality made it so. The population profile of the twentieth century has been very different. With certain exceptions such as the 'baby boom' after the Second World War, fertility has declined; and at certain periods there has been concern about the issue of population decline. Beveridge (Cmd. 6404, para. 413) reflected such a mood with his stark assertion, that 'with its present rate of reproduction, the British population cannot survive'. Such a perception became an important ingredient in his advocacy of children's allowances which could help restore the birth rate 'both by making it possible for parents who desire more children to bring them into the world without damaging the chances of those already born, and as a signal of the national interest in children'.

Matching the decline of fertility, there has also been an increased rate of life expectancy which has significantly extended and improved over the course of the century. Whereas during the course of the nineteenth century life expectancy at birth increased by about 11 years, its rise in the twentieth century has been over 26 years, although significant social class differentials have remained (Tranter, 1996, p. xiv). The consequence of such demographic trends has been a 'greying' of the population. Whereas in 1901 5 per cent (1 in 20) lived beyond the age of 65, the figure is now almost 20 per cent (or 1 in 5) of the population. Compared to the beginning of the century when the age structure of the population resembled a pyramid, its more recent characteristic has been increasingly rectangular (Jeffreys and Thane, 1989, p. 1).

Furthermore, distinctions are now commonly made between the 'young old' (65–74) and the 'old' (75–84) and the 'very old' (85+). Meanwhile, predictions show an upward trajectory up to 2031 of those over pensionable age, though in the short term it is the absolute growth of the 'very old' that is usually highlighted. It is not only the growing number and proportion of older people that has led some commentators to talk of a demographic 'time bomb' threatening an unsustainable level of welfare costs. That trend is also related to the simultaneous reduction in the numbers of those in the active labour force. The interplay of these factors is generally considered to have an especial impact on a predominantly 'pay as you go' pensions policy and on the funding of health and social care services. Hills (1993, p. 78), however, has argued that the options for public spending are wider than such a scenario might suggest, and that 'the future performance of the economy and the level of unemployment in particular will have as great an effect as demography itself'.

Changes in the population profile have been part of the reason for a renewed interest in the life-cycle and especially for a concentration on older age. Another has been the way in which the alternative distributive mechanisms of work and welfare have altered over the course of the century. Active labour force participation has become concentrated into a shorter time span. This is the result both of the extension of schooling delaying entry into work, and the introduction of fixed ages at which retirement pensions are payable. Its effect has been to create a three-stage model of the conventional life-course separated into childhood, paid employment, and retirement. It has been suggested on the one hand that such a model over-emphasizes the distinctiveness of the twentieth-century experience and, on the other, that it also needs to take account of adolescence, early retirement and unpaid work. Johnson (1989, p. 62) meanwhile has questioned the tendency to automatically equate the periods of childhood and retirement with dependency, arguing that the structured dependency thesis of Townsend and Walker has 'deflected attention from the more progressive and optimistic views of the economic [and] social status of the elderly in modern Britain'. The notion of dependency, however, is not only contestable; it is also multi-faceted. This discussion is confined to the related dimensions of employment change and financial support.

Compulsory schooling between the ages of five and 10 was introduced in 1880. Thereafter the length of schooling became progressively prolonged: to 12 in 1899, 14 in 1918, 15 in 1947 and 16 in 1972. 'By compulsorily keeping children within the classroom, schooling lengthened the years of "childhood" while simultaneously reinforcing notions of the characteristics that were said to constitute proper childhood, namely ignorance, innocence and dependence' (Hendrick, 1997, p. 64). For some (Humphries, 1988, p. 30) this changing status was symbolized by the payment of pocket money rather than wages. Compulsory schooling also meant that for working-class families especially, children became more of an economic liability than an asset. Not only were they progressively excluded from paid employment, they were also less available for domestic work and the care of young siblings (Fox Harding, 1996, pp. 173–4).

More recent trends have reinforced the process. As preparation for entry into the labour market takes longer, so young people remain dependent on their parents for longer. An increasing proportion of young people continue beyond school into higher education. In the 1950s it was 5 per cent of the age group; it is now about one-third. For many others, special employment schemes and youth training programmes have become a lengthening and controversial bridge between school and work. Meanwhile, since the late 1980s 16-to 18-year-olds have been largely excluded from the social security system and expected to continue to rely on their parents if they are unable to find paid work. Thereafter until the age of 25 young people's entitlement to social security support remains restricted. Over the same period, publicly provided financial support for students in higher education has also been reduced.

If children and young people have been progressively excluded from the world of paid employment, it has been suggested that the introduction of retirement policies has produced a similar marginalization of older people. State-provided old age pensions were introduced in 1908 and became part of the National Insurance scheme in 1925 at which time the pension age was reduced from 70 to 65. It was not until 1948 that the concept of mandatory retirement was introduced with the establishment of universal public pensions. Payable at the age of 65 for men and 60 for women (the age to which it was reduced in 1940), these pension ages became the threshold of old age and increasingly the point of withdrawal from paid employment. Paradoxically, the Second World War had witnessed an increase in employment for older workers and Beveridge, concerned to save on pension costs, argued that 'making receipt of pension conditional on retirement is not intended to encourage or hasten retirement' (Cmd. 6404, para. 245). It was a view echoed, primarily on the grounds of cost, in the Report of the Royal Commission on Population (1949) and in the Phillips Report (1954) which recommended raising the retirement age to 67 (Phillipson, 1994, p. 136).

Increasingly, however, the tendency for men over 65 to be in paid employment has declined. Between 1951 and 1994 their labour force participation rate reduced from just over 30 per cent to 7.5 per cent. In the earlier part of this period special measures designed to retain older workers in the labour force declined in importance 'as the supply of younger people increased, as immigration grew, and as greater numbers of women entered the labour market' (Taylor and Walker, 1996, p. 161). Meanwhile, in the economic recession of the 1970s and 1980s there were inducements such as the Job Release Scheme and redundancy payments which encouraged early retirement and the substitution of younger for older workers. Between the mid-1970s and the mid-1990s the percentage of men aged 60 to 64 who were in paid employment declined from 82.3 to 51.2 per cent. As Alan Walker (1997a, p. 251) has noted:

it is now only a minority of men that 'retire' in the conventional sense of leaving work on or close to their sixty-fifth birthday. The majority leave employment at earlier ages and reach the statutory pension age in a variety of non-employed statuses, such as unemployment, long-term sickness and disability and early retirement.

The corollary of the social process of retirement and withdrawal from the labour market is that older people are increasingly dependent on the state for financial support. This does not apply to all older people, however. As Beveridge (Cmd. 6404, para. 235) noted '[o]ld age may cause acute poverty or it may cause no poverty at all'. The distinction between the 'two nations' in old age has persisted over the past 50 years. It is a distinction between those on the one hand who are dependent on state-provided financial support and, on the other, those who have other sources of income in old age which result from a lifetime's secure employment and savings, occupational pensions and the ownership of a house. This latter group have recently been characterized as WOOPIES (Well Off Older People) and several niche markets (in leisure, recreation and clothing, for example) have developed especially for such affluent older people.

Throughout the twentieth century, however, older people have also been one of the largest groups living in poverty. In Rowntree's first study of York it was old age along with childhood that constituted the greatest risk. By the time of his second report in 1936, 'poverty due to old age was more acute than that due to any other single cause' (Cmd. 6404, para. 235). Despite the introduction of universal pensions, successive research has pointed to the persistence of poverty in old age. In the early 1980s, for example, Walker and Hutton (1988, p. 47) estimated that 70 per cent of pensioner households were living in or on the margins of poverty; while in 1994/5 retired households were dependent on social security benefits for an average of 51 per cent of their household income, in contrast to 13 per cent of all households (HMSO 1995)

The inequalities of old age not only occur between the WOOPIES and those dependent on financial support, there are also significant varieties of experience within the latter group. Successive research studies have highlighted the greater incidence of poverty among single pensioners, the majority of whom are women and who tend on average to be older than other groups of pensioners. In 1994 even after adjusting for their different retirement ages 'there were over five times as many women pensioners as men dependent on income support' (Oppenheim and Harker, 1996, p. 61). While the average weekly household disposable income was about £300 per week, for single pensioners it was £79. The fact that women pensioners are at greater risk of financial insecurity than either married pensioner couples or pensioner men is the result of the interplay of several factors. Among these are their lower earnings, interrupted work patterns, discriminatory pensions practices, lesser likelihood of occupational pensions and their greater life expectancy. In such ways do the experiences of earlier life – whether in or out of the labour market – condition life chances in retirement.

The introduction and prolongation of compulsory schooling also carried financial implications since family finances had to be spread over a longer period of dependency. Children, that is to say, not only increased family costs: in addition their value as a source of income was reduced, though some part-time work and errands remained a means of earning a few pence (Vincent, 1991, p. 19). It is not surprising, therefore, that families with children featured as one of the principal categories in Rowntree's account of the life-cycle of poverty. The super-imposition of the life-cycle of need onto a family's typical lifetime income 'graphically showed the gap between income and the needs of families in the child rearing years, especially for the poorest' (Glennerster, 1995b, p. 11).

The emergent solution to this problem of family resources was two-fold: the idea of a minimum wage which Rowntree himself favoured, but which was fraught with methodological difficulties in its calculation; or a system of family endowment which would specifically recognize the costs of children. Its prototype were the allowances paid in respect of children during the First World War to women whose husbands were in the services. During the interwar years Eleanor Rathbone provided a powerful influence for the introduction of such a scheme, but 'she struggled in vain to overcome the ingrained conservatism of the trade unions' whose leaders remained 'committed to solving child poverty by gaining for the male wage earner an income sufficient to support all his dependants without further subvention from the state' (Vincent, 1991, p. 64).

Child allowances were one of the basic assumptions of the Beveridge Report. But the decisive factor in their introduction was the recognition of the disincentive effect that would be created 'if the social security scheme was to give cash support to unemployed workers' families in a way that reflected the number of children in the family'. Under such circumstances the Treasury recognized that 'many unemployed people would be better off financially out of work rather than in work' (Glennerster, 1995a, p. 12). In this way the relationship between work and welfare shaped the nature of family allowances as a universal and unconditional benefit. Subsequently renamed Child Benefit and extended to cover the first child, it is 'unique in that it recognises the cost of rearing children unconditionally and, though small, is an essential element in the income of many mothers' (Fox Harding, 1996, p. 132). Though it does not – and was not intended to – cover the total cost involved in bringing up a child, its strategic importance especially to low-income households has led to concern when its level has been behind inflation or frozen for a number of years at a particular level.

On the other hand, there are those who argue that by means-testing the benefit, it could be targeted more effectively at those who need it most. This is part of a long-standing debate within twentieth-century social policy between those supporting universal benefits with their high level of take-up and their symbolic recognition of shared risks, and the advocates of a strategically targeted use of resources in order to offset the disadvantages, risks and costs of particular individuals and groups and of particular periods in the life-cycle. The present Labour government has committed itself to maintaining child benefit on a universal basis, though it has suggested (Cm. 3805, p. 58) that future increases will be met by higher-rate taxpayers paying tax on it.

Conclusion

This chapter has suggested that within the welfare state existing inequalities (such as those based on gender and class) have remained, while new divisions based on generation (as well as race) have developed. For a considerable body of social policy opinion that constitutes the apparent failure of the welfare state to realize its objectives of creating greater integration and a more solidaristic society. For others, its failure to bring about a more equal society is:

balanced by its success in nurturing a more prosperous one, in which the rich and powerful were not really threatened, in which the middle classes experienced, without fully recognising it, great benefits from the new social programmes and in which working people felt largely content that their world was improving. (Williamson, 1990, p. 86)

While opinions about outcomes differ, there is general agreement that Britain's welfare system at the end of the twentieth century is in many respects different to what it was at the beginning. State activity is more comprehensive, the range of benefits and services is wider, and the principle of welfarism retains a certain established legitimacy. All of that is in sharp contrast to what might well have been predicted a century ago: 'that the provision of social welfare in Britain was and would continue to be highly localised, amateur, voluntaristic and intimate in scale...' (Harris, 1992b, p. 116). That perception underlines the significance of the expansionary role of state activity in the first three-quarters of the twentieth century. And it is tempting in taking the long view to follow Paci's (1987, p. 194) analysis which suggests that

> if in the almost forty years from the National Insurance Bill of 1911 and the postwar legislation the state reduced the scope of the private economy in the provision of social protection, in the almost forty years since we have witnessed a sort of 'revenge of the market'.

The issues in both periods may be more complex and diverse than such a general analysis permits. But such a perspective does enable us to hold in tension two recent assessments of the welfare state. The first is the view that despite the 'economic hurricane' of the 1970s and the 'ideological blizzard' of the 1980s what was remarkable about the welfare state in the early 1990s was 'how much, not how little remained' (Timmins, 1995, p. 503). The second view argues the importance of the mid-1970s as a critical turning point in Britain's welfare state. Thereafter it ceased to be expansionary. It is 'welfare with the lid on' (Glennerster, 1998, p. 308) that has characterized the past 20 years – with a constraint on spending as demand increased – especially from the unemployed and the no longer employed – and expectations rose. 'It is not merely that the lid has been put on but that the steam pressure in the pot has been rising too' (*ibid.*, p. 311).

At the micro-level of individual services, the picture is diverse. In income maintenance, for example, the welfare state appears to have better fulfilled Beveridge's aim of redistributing resources across the life-cycle than acting as an agent of redistribution *per se*. The model is thus akin to that of a savings bank in which 'three quarters of all the taxes that people pay come back to them individually but at different times in their lives. Only a quarter of the total goes to others' (Glennerster, 1995a, p. 227). In health care, the NHS despite the well-attested continuing disadvantages of vulnerable groups, represents 'an enormous improvement on the ramshackle assemblage of health services that it superseded' (Webster, 1998, p. 215): while education has a creditable record of expanding opportunity despite the fact that it 'has failed to keep Britain competitive with its industrial neighbours' (Sanderson, 1994, p. 389). Over the century the pattern of housing tenure has changed dramatically. Whereas at its beginning most of the population rented from a private landlord, at the century's end Britain has one of the highest rates of home ownership. Local authority or 'council' housing meanwhile has been progressively residualized, while the role of housing associations in the supply of social housing has increased. The personal social services remain the best exemplar of the 'mixed economy of welfare', but in this sector over the past 100 years there has been a continuing – and at times expanding – statutory responsibility for children, disabled and older people.

But as this study has been at pains to show, the state's role in welfare during the twentieth century has not been the whole story. Some agents of welfare supply have declined – such as the organizations of working-class self-help and mutual aid – while others, such as the private market, have increased, at least in selected sectors of welfare. Some have reinvented themselves such as happened in the voluntary sector in the 1960s, while others such as the independent or 'public' schools have retained much of their traditional role. In many respects the changing role of these other sources of welfare supply has been the result of political decisions about the acceptable and legitimate role of the state. At certain times and for certain services, it may have 'crowded out' other providers; at others it has brought them back in and reasserted their position in the welfare matrix, often with state-provided subsidies. The pattern has thus been one of change and continuity within sectors and between sectors.

As much current historical writing recognizes, such a perspective offers a more dynamic approach to the study of the past of social welfare. In place of an historical inevitability concerning the role of the state and the fundamental divide between public and other providers, assumed by earlier historians, the new history of welfare is constructed from the variety of agencies engaged in providing protection against risks and their changing interrelationship over time.

Such an approach suggestively also forms an emergent agenda for the politics of welfare towards the end of the twentieth century and 50 years on from the creation of the classic welfare state. As they have been for much of this century, political decisions about the respective responsibilities of the state, other agencies and of individuals remain central to the creation of any welfare settlement or contract. Though such decisions are located within the structures of contemporary discourse – work and welfare, benefits and behaviour, for example – they are also located within a set of ideas, institutions and expectations inherited from the past. There is no *tabula rasa* in Britain's welfare state. That may constrain the available range of options both for tax and spend than more radical politicians – either of the Left or the Right – would wish. But it suggests for the future, as for the past century, the likelihood of continuing change among providers within the mixed economy of welfare.

*   *   *

There always has been, and always will be, both a gulf between policy and performance and a gap between well-being and welfare; but the verdict to be passed on the policy-makers at the end of day is up to you. (W.G. Runciman, 1997)

BIBLIOGRAPHY

Abel-Smith, B. (1958) 'Whose Welfare State?', in Norman Mackenzie (ed.), *Conviction* (London: MacGibbon & Kee).

Addison, P. (1975) *The Road to 1945* (London: Jonathan Cape).

Addison, P. (1985) *Now the War is Over: A Social History of Britain 1945–51* (London: BBC and Jonathan Cape).

Addison, P. (1987) 'The Road from 1945', in Peter Hennessy and Anthony Seldon (eds), *Ruling Performance* (Oxford: Basil Blackwell).

Addison, P. (1993) *Churchill on the Home Front 1900–1955* (London: Pimlico).

Alt, J. E. (1979) *The Politics of Economic Decline* (Cambridge: Cambridge University Press).

Alberti, J. (1996) *Eleanor Rathbone* (London: Sage).

Alcock, P. (1996) *Social Policy in Britain* (London: Macmillan).

Armstrong, W. A. (1990) 'The Countryside', in F. M. L. Thompson (ed.), *The Cambridge Social History of Britain 1750–1950*, Vol. 1 (Cambridge: Cambridge University Press).

Ashford, D. E. (1986) *The Emergence of the Welfare States* (Oxford: Basil Blackwell).

Audit Commission (1989) *Losing an Empire, Finding a Role* (London: HMSO).

Bacon, R. and Eltis, W. (1978) *Britain's Economic Problem: Too Few Producers* (London: Macmillan).

Baldwin, P. (1990) *The Politics of Social Solidarity: Class Bases of the European Welfare State 1875–1975* (Cambridge: Cambridge University Press).

Barker, R. (1997) *Political Ideas in Modern Britain* (London: Routledge).

Barnett, C. (1986) *The Audit of War* (London: Macmillan).

Bell, D. (1960) *The End of Ideology* (Chicago: Chicago University Press).

Bellamy, C. (1988) *Administering Central–Local Relations 1871–1919* (Manchester: Manchester University Press).

Benn, C. (1980) 'Comprehensive School Reform and the 1945 Labour Government', *History Workshop Journal*, 10, pp. 197–204.

Beresford, P. (1997) 'The Last Social Division? Revisiting the Relationship between Social Policy, its Producers and Consumers', in M. May, E. Brundson and G. Craig (eds), *Social Policy Review*, 9, Social Policy Association.

Bonham, J. (1954) *The Middle Class Voter* (London: Faber & Faber).

Bourke, J. (1994) *Working Class Cultures in Britain 1890–1960* (London: Routledge).

Braithwaite, C. (1938) *The Voluntary Citizen: An Enquiry into the Place of Philanthropy in the Community* (London: Methuen).

Brenton, M. (1985) *The Voluntary Sector in British Social Services* (London: Longman).

Brook, L. *et al.* (1996) 'Public Spending and Taxation', in Roger Jowell *et al.* (eds), *British Social Attitudes: The 13th Report* (Aldershot: Dartmouth).

Brooke, S. (1991) 'The Labour Party and the Second World War', in Anthony Gorst (ed), *Contemporary British History 1931–1961* (London: Pinter).

Brooke, S. (1992) *Labour's War: The Labour Party during the Second World War* (Oxford: Clarendon Press).

Brown, R. G. S. (1975) *The Management of Welfare* (London: Fontana).

Brunsdon, E. (1997) 'Private Welfare', in Pete Alcock, A. Erskine and M. May (eds), *The Student's Companion to Social Policy* (Oxford: Blackwell).

Burk, K. (1982) *War and the State: The Transformation of British Government, 1914–1919* (London: Allen & Unwin).

Butcher, H. *et al.* (1990) *Local Government and Thatcherism* (London: Routledge).

Butcher, T. (1995) *Delivering Welfare: The Governance of the Social Services in the 1990s* (Buckingham: Open University Press).

Butler, D. and Stokes, D. (1974) *Political Change in Britain*, 2nd edn (London: Macmillan).

Calder, A. (1991) *The Myth of the Blitz* (London: Jonathan Cape).

Ceadel, M. (1991) 'Labour as a Governing Party: Balancing Right and Left', in T. Gourvish and A. O'Day (eds), *Britain Since 1945* (London: Macmillan).

Chamberlain, J. (1914) *Mr Chamberlain's Speeches*, ed. C. W. Boyd (London: Constable).

Charmley, J. (1996) *A History of Conservative Politics, 1900–1996* (London: Macmillan).

Clarke, J., A. Cochrane and E. McLaughlin (eds) (1994) *Managing Social Policy* (London: Sage).

Clarke, J. and Newman, J. (1997) *The Managerial State* (London: Sage).

Clarke, P. (1992) *A Question of Leadership: From Gladstone to Thatcher* (Harmondsworth: Penguin).

Clarke, P. (1996) *Hope and Glory: Britain 1900–1990* (Harmondsworth: Allen Lane, The Penguin Press).

Cm. 555 (1989) *Working for Patients* (London: HMSO).

Cm. 1730 (1991) *Competing for Quality* (London: HMSO).

Cm. 2101 (1992) *The Citizens' Charter: First Report* (London: HMSO).

Cm. 3805 (1998) *A New Contract for Welfare* (London: HMSO).

Cmd. 5609 (1937) *The Public Social Services* (London: HMSO).

Cmd. 6404 (1942) *Social Insurance and Allied Services*, Report by Sir William Beveridge (London: HMSO).

Cmnd. 7746 (1979) *The Government's Expenditure Plans 1980–81* (London: HMSO).

Coates, D. (1980) *Labour in Power? A Study of the Labour Government 1974–1979* (London: Longman).

Cockett, R. (1995) *Thinking the Unthinkable: Think-Tanks and the Economic Counter-Revolution 1931–1983* (London: HarperCollins).

Cole, G. D. H. and Cole, M. I. (1937) *The Condition of Britain* (London: Victor Gollancz).

Cooter, R. (1992) *In the Name of the Child* (London: Routledge).

Cousins, C. (1987) *Controlling Social Welfare* (Brighton: Harvester Wheatsheaf).

Craig, F. W. S. (ed.) (1975) *British General Education Manifestos 1900–1974* (London: Macmillan).

Crewe, I. (1996) '1979–1996', in Anthony Seldon (ed.), *How Tory Governments Fail* (London: Fontana).

Cronin, J. E. (1988) 'The British State and the Structure of Political Opportunity', *Journal of British Studies*, 27, pp. 199–231.

Cronin, J. E. (1991) *The Politics of State Expansion* (London: Routledge).

Crosland, C. A. R. (1962) *The Conservative Enemy* (London: Jonathan Cape).

Crossman, R. H. S. (1976) 'The Role of the Volunteer in Modern Social Service', in A. H. Halsey (ed.), *Traditions of Social Policy* (Oxford: Basil Blackwell).

Crowther, A. (1988) *British Social Policy 1914–1939* (London: Macmillan).

Crowther, M. A. (1982) 'Family Responsibility and State Responsibility in Britain before the Welfare State', *Historical Journal* 25(1), pp. 131–45.

D'Cruze, S. (1995) 'Women and the Family', in J. Purvis (ed.), *Women's History: Britain 1850–1945* (London: University College London. Press).

Dalton, H. (1962) *High Tide and After* (London: Muller).

Daunton, M. (1996a) 'Introduction', in Martin Daunton (ed.), *Charity, Self-Interest and Welfare in the English Past* (London: UCL Press).

Daunton, M. (1996b) 'Payment and Participation: Welfare and State-Formation in Britain 1900–1951, *Past and Present*, 150, pp. 169–216.

Davis Smith, J. *et al.* (1995) *An Introduction to the Voluntary Sector* (London: Routledge).

Deacon, A. (1982) 'An End to the Means Test? Social Security and the Attlee Government', *Journal of Social Policy*, 11(3), pp. 289–306.

Deacon, A. (1987) 'Systems of Interwar Unemployment Relief', in Sean Glynn and Alan Booth (eds), *The Road to Full Employment* (London: Allen & Unwin).

Deacon, A. (1995) 'Spending More to Achieve Less?: Social Security since 1945', in David Gladstone (ed.), *British Social Welfare: Past, Present and Future* (London: UCL Press).

Deacon, A. and Bradshaw, J. (1983) *Reserved for the Poor: The Means Test in British Social Policy* (Oxford: Basil Blackwell and Martin Robertson).

Deakin, N. (1985) 'Local Government and Social Policy', in Martin Loughlin, M. D. Gelf and and K. Young (eds), *Half a Century of Municipal Decline* (London: George Allen & Unwin).

Deakin, N. (1988) *In Search of the Postwar Consensus*, Welfare State Programme, London School of Economics.

Deakin, N. (1994) *The Politics of Welfare* (Hemel Hempstead: Harvester Wheatsheaf).

Deakin, N. (1995) 'The Perils of Partnership', in J. Davis Smith, C. Rochester and R. Hedley (eds), *An Introduction to the Voluntary Sector* (London: Routledge).

Deakin, N. and Wright, A. (1990) *Consuming Public Services* (London: Routledge).

De Groot, G. J. (1996) *Blighty: British Society in the Era of the Great War* (London: Longman).

Dewey, P. (1997) *War and Progress: Britain 1914–1945* (London: Longman).

Digby, A. (1989) *British Welfare Policy: Workhouse to Workfare* (London: Faber & Faber).

Digby, A. and Stewart, J. (1996) 'Welfare in Context', in Anne Digby and John Stewart (eds), *Gender, Health and Welfare* (London: Routledge).

Dingwall, R. *et al.* (1988) *An Introduction to the Social History of Nursing* (London: Routledge).

Donnison, D. (1982) *The Politics of Poverty* (Oxford: Martin Robertson).

Donoughue, B. (1987) *Prime Minister: The Conduct of Policy under Harold Wilson and James Callaghan* (London: Jonathan Cape).

Donzelot, J. (1980) *The Policing of Families* (London: Hutchinson).

Dorey, P. (1995) *British Politics since 1945* (Oxford: Blackwell).

Dutton, D. (1997) *British Politics since 1945* (Oxford: Blackwell).

Dwork, D. (1987) *War is Good for Babies and Other Young Children* (London: Tavistock).

Ellison, N. (1997) 'From Welfare State to Post-Welfare Society? Labour's Social Policy in Historical and Contemporary Perspective', in Brian Brivati and Tim Bale (eds), *New Labour in Power* (London: Routledge).

Esping-Andersen, G. (1990) *The Three Worlds of Welfare Capitalism* (Cambridge: Cambridge University Press).

Esping-Andersen, G. (1996) *Welfare States in Transition* (London: Sage).

Evandrou, M. and Falkingham, J. (1995) 'Gender, Lone-parenthood and Lifetime Incomes', in J. Falkingham and J. Hills (eds), *The Dynamic of Welfare* (Hemel Hempstead: Prentice Hall).

Evans, E. J. (1997) *Thatcher and Thatcherism* (London: Routledge).

Falush, P. (1977) 'Trends in the Finance of British Charities', *National Westminster Bank Quarterly Review* May, pp. 32–44.

Feinstein, C. H. (1972) *Statistical Tables of National Income, Expenditure and Output of the U.K. 1855–1965* (Cambridge: Cambridge University Press).

Field, F. (1973) *Unequal Britain* (London: Arrow).

Field, F. (1997) *Reforming Welfare* (London: Social Market Foundation).

Fielding, S. (1992) 'What Did "the People" Want? The Meaning of the 1945 General Election', *Historical Journal*, 25(3), pp. 623–39.

Finch, J. (1989) *Family Obligations and Social Change* (London: Polity Press).

Finch, J. and Groves, D. (1980) 'Community Care and the Family: A Case for Equal Opportunities', *Journal of Social Policy*, 9(4), pp. 487–512.

Finlayson, G. (1990) 'A Moving Frontier: Voluntarism and the State in British Social Welfare, 1911–1949', *Twentieth Century British History*, 1(2), pp. 183–206.

Finlayson, G. (1994) *Citizen, State and Social Welfare in Britain 1830–1990* (Oxford: Clarendon Press).

Flynn, N. (1997) *Public Sector Management*, 3rd edn (Hemel Hempstead: Prentice Hall).

Forrest, R. and Murie, A. (1988) *Selling the Welfare State* (London: Routledge).

Fox Harding, L. (1996) *Family, State and Social Policy* (London: Macmillan).

Francis, M. (1996a) 'Set the People Free? Conservatives and the State 1920–1960', in Martin Francis and Ina Zweiniger-Bargielowska (eds), *The Conservatives and British Society 1880–1990* (Cardiff: University of Wales Press).

Francis, M. (1996b) 'Not Reformed Capitalism, But ... Democratic Socialism: The Ideology of the Labour Leadership 1945–1951', in Harriet Jones and Michael Kandiah (eds), *The Myth of Consensus* (London: Macmillan).

Francis, M. (1997) *Ideas and Policies under Labour, 1945–1951: Building a New Britain* (Manchester: Manchester University Press).

Fraser, D. (1984) *The Evolution of the British Welfare State* (London: Macmillan).

Freeden, M. (1990) 'The Stranger at the Feast: Ideology and Public Policy in Twentieth Century Britain', *Twentieth Century British History*, 1(1), pp. 9–34.

Gamble, A. (1988) *The Free Economy and the Strong State* (London: Macmillan).

Garside, W. R. (1990) *British Unemployment 1919–1939* (Cambridge: Cambridge University Press).

Gilbert, B. B. (1970) *British Social Policy 1914–1939* (London: B. T. Batsford).

Gladstone, D. (1995), 'The Welfare State and the State of Welfare', In David Gladstone (ed.) *British Social Welfare: Past, Present and Future* (London: UCL Press).

Glennerster, H. (1990) 'Social Policy since the Second World War', in J. Hills (ed.), *The State of Welfare* (Oxford: Clarendon Press).

Glennerster, H. (1992a) *Paying for Welfare* (Hemel Hempstead: Harvester Wheatsheaf).

Glennerster, H. (1992b) *Paying for Welfare: Issues for the Nineties*, Welfare State Programme, London School of Economics.

Glennerster, H. (1995a) *British Social Policy since 1945* (Oxford: Blackwell).

Glennerster, H. (1995b) 'The Life Cycle: Public or Private Concern?', in Jane Falkingham and John Hills (eds), *The Dynamic of Welfare* (Hemel Hempstead: Prentice Hall).

Glennerster, H. (1998) 'Welfare with the Lid On', in Howard Glennerster (ed.), *The State of Welfare*, 2nd edn (Oxford: Oxford University Press).

Glennerster, H. and Evans, M. (1994) 'Beveridge and his Assumptive Worlds', in John Hills *et al.* (eds), *Beveridge and Social Security* (Oxford: Clarendon Press).

Glynn, S. and Booth, A. (1996) *Modern Britain* (London: Routledge).

Golding, P. and Middleton, S. (1982) *Images of Welfare* (Oxford: Martin Robertson).

Goldthorpe, J. H. *et al.* (1969) *The Affluent Worker in the Class Structure* (Cambridge: Cambridge University Press).

Goldthorpe, J. H. (1980) *Social Mobility and Class Structure in Modern Britain* (Oxford: Oxford University Press).

Goodman, A. *et al.* (1997) *Inequality in the UK* (Oxford: Oxford University Press).

Gough, I. (1979) *The Political Economy of the Welfare State* (London: Macmillan).

Gowing, M. (1975) *Richard Morris Titmuss* Proceedings of the British Academy, LXI

Green, D. and Lucas, D. (1992) 'Private Welfare in the 1980s', in Nick Manning and Robert Page (eds), *Social Policy Review*, 4 (Canterbury: Social Policy Association).

Green, E. H. H. (1995) *The Crisis of Conservatism 1880–1914* (London: Routledge).

Green, E. H. H. (1996) 'The Conservative Party, the State and Social Policy, 1880–1914', in Martin Francis and Ina Zweiniger-Bargielowska (eds), *The Conservatives and British Society, 1880–1990* (Cardiff: University of Wales Press).

Greenleaf, W. H. (1983) *The British Political Tradition*, Vol. 2 (London: Methuen).

Hall, S. (1979) 'The Great Moving Right Show', in S. Hall and M. Jacques (eds), *The Politics of Thatcherism* (London: Lawrence & Wishart).

Hall, S. (1985) 'Authoritarian Populism: A Reply', *New Left Review* 151, pp.106–13.

Hannah, L. (1986) *Inventing Retirement: The Development of Occupational Pensions in Britain* (Cambridge: Cambridge University Press).

Harris, B. (1994) 'Unemployment and the Dole in Interwar Britain', in Paul Johnson (ed.), *Twentieth Century Britain* (London: Longman).

Harris, B. (1995a) *The Health of the Schoolchild: A History of the School Medical Service in England and Wales* (Buckingham: Open University Press).

Harris, B. (1995b) 'Responding to Adversity: Government–Charity Relations and the Relief of Unemployment in Inter-war Britain', *Contemporary Record*, 9(3), pp. 529–61.

Harris, J. (1972) *Unemployment and Politics: A Study in English Social Policy 1886–1914* (Oxford: Clarendon Press).

Harris, J. (1977) *William Beveridge: A Biography* (Oxford: Clarendon Press).

Harris, J. (1983a) 'The Transition to High Politics in English Social Policy 1880–1914', in Michael Bentley and John Stevenson (eds), *High and Low Politics in Modern Britain* (Oxford: Clarendon Press).

Harris, J. (1983b) 'Did British Workers Want the Welfare State?', in Jay Winter (ed.), *The Working Class in Modern British History* (Cambridge: Cambridge University Press).

Harris, J. (1990) 'Society and the State in Twentieth Century Britain', in F. M. L. Thompson (ed.), *The Cambridge Social History of Britain 1750–1950*, Vol. 3 (Cambridge: Cambridge University Press).

Harris, J. (1991) 'Enterprise and the Welfare State: A Comparative Perspective', in T. Gourvish and A. O'Day (eds), *Britain Since 1945* (London: Macmillan).

Harris, J. (1992a) 'Victorian Values and the Founders of the Welfare State', in T. C. Smout (ed.), *Victorian Values* (Oxford: Oxford University Press).

Harris, J. (1992b) 'Political Thought and the Welfare State, 1870–1940: An Intellectual Framework for British Social Policy', *Past and Present*, no. 135, pp. 116–41.

Harris, J. (1993) *Private Lives, Public Spirit: A Social History of Britain 1870–1914* (Oxford: Oxford University Press).

Harris, J. (1994) 'Beveridge's Social and Political Thought', in John Hills *et al.* (eds), *Beveridge and Social Security* (Oxford: Clarendon Press).

Harrison, B. (1996) *The Transformation of British Politics 1860–1995* (Oxford: Oxford University Press).

Hattersley, R. (1997) *Fifty Years On* (London: Little, Brown and Co.).

Hay, C. (1996) *Re-Stating Social and Political Change* (Buckingham: Open University Press).

Hay, R. (1977) 'Employers and Social Policy in Britain: The Evolution of Welfare Legislation, 1905–1914', *Social History*, 4, pp. 435–55.

Hay, R. (1978) 'Employers' Attitudes to Social Policy and the Concept of Social Control', in Pat Thane (ed.), *The Origins of British Social Policy* (London: Croom Helm).

Hayek, F. (1944) *The Road to Serfdom* (London: Routledge & Kegan Paul).

Heclo, H. and Wildavsky, A. (1981) *The Private Government of Public Money* (London: Macmillan).

Hendrick, H. (1994) *Child Welfare: England 1872–1989* (London: Routledge).

Hendrick, H. (1997) *Children, Childhood and English Society 1880–1990* (Cambridge: Cambridge University Press).

Hennessy, P. (1993) *Never Again: Britain 1945–1951* (London: Vintage).

Hennessy, P. (1996) *The Hidden Wiring* (London: Indigo).

Hennock, E. P. (1994) 'Poverty and Social Reforms', in Paul Johnson (ed.), *Twentieth Century Britain* (London: Longman).

Hill, M. (1990) *Social Security Policy in Britain* (Aldershot: Edward Elgar).

Hill, M. (1993) *The Welfare State in Britain: A Political History Since 1945* (Aldershot: Edward Elgar).

Hills, J. (1993) *The State of Welfare* (York: Joseph Rowntree Foundation).

Hills, J. (1996a) 'Tax Policy: Are There Still Choices?', in David Halpern *et al.* (eds), *Options for Britain* (Aldershot: Dartmouth).

Hills, J. (1996b) 'Introduction', in John Hills (ed.), *New Inequalities: The Changing Distribution of Income and Wealth in the UK* (Cambridge: Cambridge University Press).

Hilton Young, E. (1924) *The System of National Finance* (London: John Murray).

HMSO (1995) *Family Spending: A Report on the Family Expenditure Survey* (London: HMSO).

Hollis, P. (1987) *Ladies Elect: Women in English Local Government 1865–1914* (Oxford: Clarendon Press).

Honingsbaum, F. (1989) *Health, Happiness and Security: the Creation of the National Health Service* (London: Routledge).

Howlett, P. (1994) 'The "Golden Age", 1955–73', in Paul Johnson (ed.), *Twentieth Century Britain* (London: Longman).

Hugman, R. (1991) *Power in Caring Professions* (London: Macmillan).

Humphries, S. (1988) *A Century of Childhood* (London: Sidgwick & Jackson).

Hutton, S. *et al.* (1998) *Consumer Views on Service Delivery in the Child Support Agency* (London: DSS Research Report).

Illich, I. (1977) *Disabling Professions* (London: Boyars).

Jackman, R. (1985) 'Local Government Finance', in Martin Loughlin, M. D. Gelfand and K. Young (eds), *Half a Century of Municipal Decline* (London: George Allen & Unwin).

Jay, D. (1937) *The Socialist Case* (London: Faber & Faber).

Jefferys, K. (1987) 'British Politics and Social Policy during the Second World War', *Historical Journal*, 30(1), pp. 123–44.

Jefferys, K. (1991) *The Churchill Coalition and Wartime Politics, 1940–1945* (Manchester: Manchester University Press).

Jefferys, M. and Thane, P. (1989) 'An Ageing Society and an Ageing People', in Margot Jeffreys (ed.), *Growing Old in the Twentieth Century* (London: Routledge).

164   Bibliography

Jessop, B. *et al.* (1988) *Thatcherism: A Tale of Two Nations* (Cambridge: Polity Press).

Johnson, N. (1991) *Reconstructing the Welfare State: A Decade of Change* (Hemel Hempstead: Harvester Wheatsheaf).

Johnson, P. (1989) 'The Structured Dependency of the Elderly', in Margot Jeffreys (ed.), *Growing Old in the Twentieth Century* (London: Routledge).

Johnson, P. (1994a) 'The Welfare State', in R. Floud and D. McCloskey (eds), *The Economic History of Britain since 1700*, Vol. 3 (Cambridge: Cambridge University Press).

Johnson, P. (1994b) 'The Role of the State in Twentieth Century Britain', in Paul Johnson (ed.), *Twentieth Century Britain* (London: Longman).

Johnson, P. (1996) 'Risk, Redistribution and Social Welfare in Britain from the Poor Law to Beveridge', in Martin Daunton (ed.), *Charity, Self-Interest and Welfare in the English Past* (London: UCL Press).

Jones, Harriet (1992) 'The Conservative Party and the Welfare State 1942–1955', unpublished doctoral thesis, University of London.

Jones, Harriet and Kandiah, M. (1996) *The Myth of Consensus: New Views on British History 1945–64* (London: Macmillan).

Jones, Helen (1994) *Health and Society in Twentieth-Century Britain* (London: Longman).

Joshi, H. and Davies, H. (1994) 'The Paid and Unpaid Roles of Women: How should Social Security Adapt?', in Sally Baldwin and Jane Falkingham (eds), *Social Security and Social Change* (Hemel Hempstead: Harvester Wheatsheaf).

Judge, K. (1981) 'State Pensions and the Growth of Social Welfare Expenditure', *Journal of Social Policy*, 10(4), pp. 503–30.

Kandiah, M. (1996) 'Conservative Leaders, Strategy – and "Consensus"? 1945–1964', in Harriet Jones and Michael Kandiah (eds), *The Myth of Consensus* (London: Macmillan).

Kavanagh, D. (1987) *Thatcherism and British Politics: The End of Consensus?* (Oxford: Oxford University Press).

Kavanagh, D. and Morris, P. (1989) *Conservative Politics from Attlee to Thatcher* (Oxford: Basil Blackwell).

Klein, R. (1995) *The New Politics of the N.H.S.* (London: Longman).

King, A. (1975) 'Overload: Problems of Governing in the 1970s', *Political Studies* 23(2), pp. 284–96.

Knight, B. (1993) *Voluntary Action* (London: HMSO).

Koven, S. and Michel, S. (1989) 'Gender and the Origins of the Welfare State', *Radical History Review*, 43.

Land, H. (1975) 'The Introduction of Family Allowances', in P. Hall *et al.* (eds), *Change, Choice and Conflict in Social Policy* (London: Heinemann).

Land, H. and Rose, H. (1985) 'Compulsory Altruism for Some or an Altruistic Society for All?', in P. Bean, J. Ferris and D. Whynes (eds), *In Defence of Welfare* (London: Tavistock).

Laski, H. (1935) *A Century of Municipal Progress 1835–1935* (London: George Allen & Unwin).

Lawrence, J. (1994) 'The First World War and its Aftermath', in Paul Johnson (ed.), *Twentieth Century Britain* (London: Longman).

Leat, D. (1995) 'Funding Matters', in Justin Davis Smith (ed.), *An Introduction to the Voluntary Sector* (London: Routledge).

Le Grand, J. (1982) *The Strategy of Equality* (London: George Allen & Unwin).

Le Grand, J. and Robinson, R. (eds) (1984) *Privatisation and the Welfare State* (London: George Allen & Unwin).

Le Grand and Bartlett, W. (1993) *Quasi-Markets and Social Policy* (London: Macmillan).

Lewis, J. (1991) *Women and Social Action in Victorian and Edwardian England* (Aldershot: Edward Elgar).

Lewis, J. (1992a) *Women in Britain since 1945* (Oxford: Blackwell).

Lewis, J. (1992b) 'Providers, "Consumers", the State and the Delivery of Health Care Services in Twentieth Century Britain', in Andrew Wear (ed.), *Medicine in Society: Historical Essays* (Cambridge: Cambridge University Press).

Lewis, J. (1993) 'Developing the Mixed Economy of Care', *Journal of Social Policy* 22(2), pp. 173–92.

Lewis, J. (1994) 'Gender, the Family and Women's Agency in the Building of "Welfare States": The British case', *Social History* 19(1), pp. 37–55.

Lewis, J. (1995) *The Voluntary Sector, the State and Social Work in Britain* (Cheltenham: Edward Elgar).

Lewis, J. (1996) 'Gender and Welfare in the Late Nineteenth and Early Twentieth Centuries', in Anne Digby and John Stewart (eds.), *Gender, Health and Welfare* (London: Routledge).

Lewis, J. and Piachaud, D. (1992) 'Women and Poverty in the Twentieth Century', in Caroling Glendinning and Jane Millar (eds), *Women and Poverty in Britain: The 1990s* (Hemel Hempstead: Harvester Wheatsheaf).

Lewis, R. and Maude, A. (1949) *The English Middle Classes* (Harmondsworth: Penguin).

Lipsey, D. (1994) 'Do We Really Want More Public Spending?', in Roger Jowell *et al.* (eds), *British Social Attitudes: The 11th Report* (Aldershot: Dartmouth).

Lowe, Rodney (1989) 'Resignation at the Treasury: The Social Services Committee and the Failure to Reform the Welfare State 1955–1957', *Journal of Social Policy* 18(4), pp. 505–26.

Lowe, Rodney (1993) *The Welfare State in Britain since 1945* (London: Macmillan).

Lowe, Rodney (1994) 'Postwar Welfare', in Paul Johnson (ed.), *Twentieth Century Britain* (London: Longman).

Lowe, Rodney (1995) 'Government', in Stephen Constantine, M. W. Kirby and M. B. Rose (eds), *The First World War in British History* (London: Edward Arnold).

Lowe, Rodney (1996a) 'The Social Policy of the Heath Government', in Stuart Ball and Anthony Seldon (eds), *The Heath Government 1970–74* (London: Longman).

Lowe, Rodney (1996b) 'The Replanning of the Welfare State, 1957–1964', in Martin Francis and Ina Zweiniger-Bargielowska (eds), *The Conservatives and British Society, 1880–1990* (Cardiff: University of Wales Press).

Lowe, Rodney (1997) 'Milestone or Millstone? The 1959–1961 Plowden Committee and its Impact on British Welfare Policy', *Historical Journal* 40(2), pp. 463–91.

Lowe, Roy (1988) *Education in the Post-war Years: A Social History* (London: Routledge).

Lowe, Roy (1997) *Schooling and Social Change 1964–1990* (London: Routledge).

Lynn, P. and Davis Smith, J. (1991) *The 1991 National Survey of Voluntary Activity in the UK* (Berkhamstead: The Volunteer Centre).

Macadam, E. (1934) *The New Philanthropy: A Study of the Relations between the Statutory and Voluntary Services* (London: Allen & Unwin).

MacDonagh, O. (1958) 'The Nineteenth Century Revolution in Government: A Re-Appraisal', *Historical Journal* 1, pp. 52–67.

MacDonagh, O. (1977) *Early Victorian Government 1830–1870* (London: Weidenfeld & Nicolson).

Macmillan, H. (1933) *Reconstruction: A Plea for a National Policy* (London: Macmillan).

Macnicol, J. (1980) *The Movement for Family Allowances* (London: Heinemann).

Macnicol, J. (1986) 'The Effect of the Evacuation of Schoolchildren on Official Attitudes to State Intervention', in Harold L. Smith (ed.), *War and Social Change: British Society in the Second World War* (Manchester: Manchester University Press).

Marquand, D. (1988a) *The Unprincipled Society* (London: Fontana Press).

Marquand, D. (1988b) 'The Paradoxes of Thatcherism', in Robert Skidelsky (ed.), *Thatcherism* (London: Chatto & Windus).

Marshall, T. H. (1950) *Citizenship and Social Class* (Cambridge: Cambridge University Press).

Marshall, T. H. (1975) *Social Policy* (London: Hutchinson).

Marwick, A. (1963) 'Middle Opinion in the Thirties: Planning, Progress and Political "Agreement"', *English Historical Review* 64, pp. 285–98.

Massey, D. (1993) *Managing the Public Sector* (Cheltenham: Edward Elgar).

Mayo, M. and Weir, A. (1993) 'The Future for Feminist Social Policy', in Robert Page and John Baldock (eds), *Social Policy Review* 5 (Canterbury: Social Policy Association).

McCallum, R. B. and Readman, A. (1947) *The General Election of 1945* (Oxford: Oxford University Press).

McCord, N. (1978) 'Ratepayers and Social Policy', in Pat Thane (ed.), *The Origins of British Social Policy* (London: Croom Helm).

McCarthy, M. (1986) *Campaigning for the Poor: CPAG and the Politics of Welfare* (London: Croom Helm).

McDowell, L. (1988) 'In Work', in Michael Ball, F. Gray and L. McDowell (eds), *The Transformation of Britain* (London: Fontana).

McKibbin, R. (1998) *Classes and Cultures: England 1918–1951* (Oxford: Oxford University Press).

Means, R. (1995) 'Older People and the Personal Social Services', in David Gladstone (ed.), *British Social Welfare: Past, Present and Future* (London: UCL Press).

Means, R. and Smith, R. (1985) *The Development of Welfare Services for Elderly People* (London: Croom Helm).

Middleton, R. (1996a) *Government versus the Market* (Cheltenham: Edward Elgar).

Middleton, R. (1996b) 'The Size and Scope of the Public Sector', in S. J. D. Green and R. C. Whiting (eds), *The Boundaries of the State in Modern Britain* (Cambridge: Cambridge University Press).

Millar, J. (1994) 'Lone Parents and Social Security Policy in the UK', in Sally Baldwin and Jane Falkingham (eds), *Social Security and Social Change* (Hemel Hempstead: Harvester Wheatsheaf).

Millar, J. (1997) 'Gender', in Alan Walker and Carol Walker (eds), *Britain Divided* (London: Child Poverty Action Group).

Mishra, R. (1984) *The Welfare State in Crisis* (Brighton: Harvester Wheatsheaf).

Moran, M. (1988) 'Crises of the Welfare State', *British Journal of Political Science* 18, pp. 397–414.

Morgan, D. and Evans, M. (1993) *The Battle for Britain: Citizenship and Ideology in the Second World War* (London: Routledge).

Morgan, K. O. (1984) *Labour in Power 1945–1951* (Oxford: Oxford University Press).

Morgan, K. O. (1990) *The People's Peace: British History 1945–1989* (Oxford: Oxford University Press).

Morgan, P. (1995) *Farewell to the Family? Public Policy and Family Breakdown* (London: Institute of Economic Affairs).

Mullard, M. (1993) *The Politics of Public Expenditure*, 2nd edn (London: Routledge).

Murie, A. (1975) *The Sale of Council Houses* (Birmingham: Centre for Urban and Regional Studies).

Murie, A. (1995) 'Housing: On the Edge of the Welfare State', in David Gladstone (ed.), *British Social Welfare: Past, Present and Future* (London: UCL Press).

Oppenheim, C. (1997a) *The Post-Conservative Welfare State* (Sheffield: Policy Paper no. 9, Political Economy Research Centre, University of Sheffield).

Oppenheim, C. (1997b) 'The Growth of Poverty and Inequality', in Alan Walker and Carol Walker (eds), *Britain Divided* (London: CPAG).

Oppenheim, C. and Harker, L. (1996) *Poverty: The Facts* (London: CPAG).

Overy, R. (1988) 'The Decline of Britain?', in Lesley M. Smith (ed.), *Echoes of Greatness* (London: Macmillan).

Paci, M. (1987) 'Long Waves in the Development of Welfare Systems', in Charles S. Maier (ed.), *Changing Boundaries of the Political* (Cambridge: Cambridge University Press).

Papadakis, E. and Taylor-Gooby, P. (1987) *The Private Provision of Public Welfare* (Brighton: Wheatsheaf Books).

Parker, H. M. D. (1957) *Manpower: A Study of War-time Policy and Administration* (London: HMSO).

Peacock, A. T. and Wiseman, J. (1967) *The Growth of Public Expenditure in the United Kingdom* (London: George Allen & Unwin).

Peden, G. C. (1991) *British Economic and Social Policy* (Hemel Hempstead: Philip Allan).

Pedersen, S. (1993) *Family, Dependence and the Origins of the Welfare State* (Cambridge: Cambridge University Press).

Pelling, H. (1980) 'The 1945 General Election Reconsidered', *The Historical Journal*, 23(2), pp. 399–414.

Perkin, H. (1989) *The Rise of Professional Society: England since 1880* (London: Routledge).

Phillips, D. R. and Vincent, J. R. (1984) 'Petit Bourgeois Care: Private Residential Care for the Elderly', *Policy and Politics*, 14(2), pp. 189–208.

Phillipson, C. (1994) 'The Modernisation of the Life Course', in Sally Baldwin and Jane Falkingham (eds), *Social Security and Social Change* (Hemel Hempstead: Harvester Wheatsheaf).

Pierson, C. (1991) *Beyond the Welfare State?* (London: Polity Press).

Pierson, C. (1996) *The Modern State* (London: Routledge).

Pimlott, B. (1988) 'The Myth of Consensus', in Lesley M. Smith (ed.), *The Making of Britain: Echoes of Greatness* (London: Macmillan).

Political and Economic Planning (PEP) (1937) *Report on British Social Services* (London: PEP).

Porter, R. (1987) *Disease, Medicine and Society in England 1550–1860* (London: Macmillan).

Powell, M. A. (1997) *Evaluating the National Health Service* (Buckingham: Open University Press).

Prochaska, F. (1988) *The Voluntary Impulse* (London: Faber & Faber).

Pugh, M. (1988) 'Popular Conservatism in Britain: Continuity and Change, 1880–1987', *Journal of British Studies*, 27, pp. 254–82.

Pugh, M. (1992) *Women and the Women's Movement in Britain 1914–1959* (London: Macmillan).

Pugh, M. (1994) *State and Society: British Political and Social History 1870–1992* (London: Edward Arnold).

Ramsden, J. (1995) *The Age of Churchill and Eden, 1940–1957* (London: Longman).

Rhodes, R. A. W. (1997) *Understanding Governance* (Buckingham: Open University Press).

Richardson, A. (1983) *Participation* (London: Routledge & Kegan Paul).

Ritschl, D. (1997) *The Politics of Planning: The Debate on Economic Planning in Britain in the 1930s* (Oxford: Clarendon Press).

Roberts, D. (1960) *Victorian Origins of the British Welfare State* (New Haven: Yale University Press).

Robson, W. A. (1933) 'The Central Domination of Local Government', *Political Quarterly*, 4(1), pp. 85–104.

Rose, R. (1989) 'Inheritance Before Choice in Public Policy', *Studies in Public Policy* University of Strathclyde.

Rowntree, B. S. (1902) *Poverty: A Study of Town Life* (London: Macmillan).

Rubinstein, D. (1979) 'Ellen Wilkinson Reconsidered', *History Workshop Journal*, 7, pp. 161–9.

Runciman, W. G. (1997) *A Treatise on Social Theory*, Vol. III (Cambridge: Cambridge University Press).

Sainsbury, D. (1994) 'Introduction', in Diane Sainsbury (ed.), *Gendering Welfare States* (London: Sage).

Sanderson, M. (1991) 'Social Equity and Industrial Need: A Dilemma of English Education since 1945', in T. Gourvish and A. O'Day (eds), *Britain Since 1945* (London: Macmillan).

Sanderson, M. (1994) 'Education and Social Mobility', in Paul Johnson (ed.), *Twentieth Century Britain* (London: Longman).

Scott, J. (1994) *Poverty and Wealth: Citizenship, Deprivation and Privilege* (London: Longman).

Searle, G. R. (1995) *Country before Party* (London: Longman).

Seldon, A. (1994) 'Conservative Century', in Anthony Seldon and Stuart Ball (eds), *Conservative Century: The Conservative Party since 1900* (Oxford: Oxford University Press).

Self, P. (1993) *Government by the Market? The Politics of Public Choice* (London: Macmillan).

Shaw, E. (1996) *The Labour Party Since 1945* (Oxford: Basil Blackwell).

Sheard, J. (1995) 'From Lady Bountiful to Active Citizen: Volunteering and the Voluntary Sector', in J. Davis Smith, C Rochester and R. Hedley (eds), *An Introduction to the Voluntary Sector* (London: Routledge).

Silburn, R. (1995) 'Beveridge', in Vic George and Robert Page (eds), *Modern Thinkers on Welfare* (Hemel Hempstead: Prentice Hall).

Simey, M. (1951) *Charitable Effort in Liverpool in the Nineteenth Century* (Liverpool: Liverpool University Press).

Simon, B. (1965) *Education and the Labour Movement* (London: Lawrence & Wishart).

Simon, B. (1991) *Education and the Social Order 1940–1990* (London: Lawrence & Wishart).

Skeffington, A. (1969) *People and Planning* (London: HMSO).

Social Trends, Government Statistical Service, HMSO.

Stevenson, J. (1984) *British Society 1914–45* (Harmondsworth: Penguin).

Stevenson, J. (1986) 'Planner's Moon? The Second World War and the Planning Movement', in Harold L. Smith (ed.), *War and Social Change* (Manchester: Manchester University Press).

Stevenson, J. (1995) 'Engendering Welfare', *Twentieth Century British History* 6(3), pp. 381–6.

Stewart, J. (1993) *Accountability to the Public* (European Policy Forum).

Sullivan, M. (1996) *The Development of the British Welfare State* (Hemel Hempstead: Harvester Wheatsheaf).

Supple, B. (1993) 'The State and Social Investigation in Britain between the World Wars', in Michael J. Lacey and Mary O. Furner (eds), *The State and Social Investigation in Britain and the United States* (Cambridge: Cambridge University Press).

Sutherland, G. (1990) 'Education', in F. M. L. Thompson (ed.), *The Cambridge Social History of Britain 1750–1950* Vol. 3 (Cambridge: Cambridge University Press).

Taylor, A. J. P. (1965) *English History 1914–1945* (Oxford: Oxford University Press).

Taylor, M. (1995) 'Voluntary Action and the State', in David Gladstone (ed.), *British Social Welfare: Past, Present and Future* (London: UCL Press).

Taylor, P. and Walker, A. (1996) 'Intergenerational Relations in the Labour Market', in Alan Walker (ed.), *The New Generational Contract* (London: UCL Press).

Taylor-Gooby, P. (1985) *Public Opinion, Ideology and State Welfare* (London: Routledge).

Taylor-Gooby, P. (1995) 'Comfortable, Marginal and Excluded', in Roger Jowell
et al. (eds), *British Social Attitudes: The 12th Report* (Aldershot: Dartmouth).

Taylor-Gooby, P. (1997) 'Equality, Rights and Social Justice', in P. Alcock,
A. Erskine and M. May (eds), *The Student's Companion to Social Policy* (Oxford:
Blackwell).

Thain, C. and Wright, M. (1990) 'Coping with Difficulty: The Treasury and
Public Expenditure 1976–1989', *Policy and Politics* 18(1), pp. 1–16.

Thane, P. (1978) 'Non-contributory Versus Insurance Pensions 1878–1908', in
Pat Thane (ed.), *The Origins of British Social Policy* (London: Croom Helm).

Thane, P. (1984) 'The Working Class and State "Welfare" in Britain, 1880–1914',
Historical Journal 27(4), pp. 877–900.

Thane, P. (1990) 'Government and Society in England and Wales 1750–1914', in
F. M. L. Thompson (ed.), *The Cambridge Social History of Britain 1750–1950*, Vol.
3 (Cambridge: Cambridge University Press).

Thane, P. (1991a) 'Visions of Gender in the Making of the British Welfare State',
in Gisela Bock and Pat Thane (eds), *Maternity and Gender Policies: Women and the
Rise of the European Welfare States, 1880s–1950s* (London: Routledge).

Thane, P. (1991b) 'Towards Equal Opportunities? Women in Britain since 1945',
in T. Gourvish and A. O'Day (eds), *Britain since 1945* (London: Macmillan).

Thane, P. (1994) 'Women since 1945', in Paul Johnson (ed.), *Twentieth Century
Britain* (London: Longman).

Thane, P. (1996) *Foundations of the Welfare State* (London: Longman).

Thompson, F. M. L. (1988) *The Rise of Respectable Society* (London: Fontana).

Thompson, N. (1996) *Political Economy and the Labour Party* (London: UCL
Press).

Thorpe, A. (1997) *A History of the British Labour Party* (London: Macmillan).

Timmins, N. (1995) *The Five Giants: A Biography of the Welfare State* (London:
HarperCollins).

Titmuss, R. M. (1950) *Problems of Social Policy* (London: HMSO and Longmans).

Titmuss, R. M. (1963) *Essays on the Welfare State* (London: George Allen &
Unwin).

Titmuss, R. M. (1987) *The Philosophy of Welfare: Selected Writings of Richard M.
Titmuss*, ed. Kay Titmuss and Brian Abel-Smith (London: Allen & Unwin).

Tomlinson, J. (1995) 'Welfare and the Economy: The Economic Impact of the
Welfare State, 1945–1951', *Twentieth Century British History* 6(2), pp. 194–219.

Tomlinson, J. (1996) ' "Liberty with Order": Conservative Economic Policy,
1951–1964', in Martin Francis and Ina Zweiniger- Bargielowska (eds),
The Conservatives and British Society, 1880–1990 (Cardiff: Cardiff University
Press).

Tomlinson, J. (1997) *Democratic Socialism and Economic Policy: The Attlee Years,
1945–1951* (Cambridge: Cambridge University Press).

Townsend, P. (1976) *Sociology and Social Policy* (Harmondsworth: Penguin).

Townsend, P. and Abel-Smith, B. (1965) *The Poor and the Poorest* (London: Bell).

Tranter, N. L. (1996) *British Population in the Twentieth Century* (London: Macmillan).

Turner, J. (1996) '1951–1964', in Anthony Seldon (ed.), *How Tory Governments Fail* (London: Fontana).

Vernon, B. D. (1982) *Ellen Wilkinson* (London: Croom Helm).

Vincent, D. (1991) *Poor Citizens: The State and the Poor in Twentieth Century Britain* (London: Longman).

Waine, B. (1992) 'The Voluntary Sector – the Thatcher Years', in Nick Manning and Robert Page (eds), *Social Policy Review* 4 (Canterbury: Social Policy Association).

Walker, A. (1986) 'Pensions and the Production of Poverty in Old Age', in Chris Phillipson and Alan Walker (eds), *Ageing and Social Policy* (Aldershot: Gower).

Walker, A. (1997a) 'Older People', in P. Alcock, A. Erskine and M. May (eds), *The Student's Companion to Social Policy* (Oxford: Blackwell).

Walker, A. (1997b) 'The Strategy of Inequality', in Alan Walker and Carol Walker (eds), *Britain Divided* (London: CPAG).

Walker, A. and Walker, C. (1987) *The Growing Divide: A Social Audit 1979–1987* (London: CPAG).

Walker, A. and Wong, C-K. (1996) 'Rethinking the Western Construction of the Welfare State', *International Journal of Health Studies* 26(1), pp. 67–92.

Walker, R. and Hutton, S. (1988) 'The Costs of Ageing and Retirement', in Robert Walker and Gillian Parker (eds), *Money Matters* (London: Sage).

Webster, C. (1988a) *The Health Services since the War*, Vol. I (London: HMSO).

Webster, C. (1988b) 'Labour and the Origins of the National Health Service', in Nicolaas A. Rupke (ed.), *Science, Politics and the Public Good* (London: Macmillan).

Webster, C. (1998) *The National Health Service: A Political History* (Oxford: Oxford University Press).

Whiteside, N. (1983) 'Private Agencies for Public Purposes', *Journal of Social Policy* 12(2), pp. 165–94.

Whiteside, N. (1991) *Bad Times: Unemployment in British Social and Political History* (London: Faber & Faber).

Whiteside, N. (1995) 'Employment Policy: A Chronicle of Decline?', in David Gladstone (ed.), *British Social Welfare: Past, Present and Future* (London: UCL Press).

Whiteside, N. (1998) 'Private Provision and Public Welfare: Health Insurance Between the Wars', in David Gladstone (ed.), *Before Beveridge: Welfare before the Welfare State* (London: IEA Health and Welfare Unit).

Whiting, R. C. (1996) 'The Boundaries of Taxation', in S. J. D. Green and R. C. Whiting (eds), *The Boundaries of the State in Modern Britain* (Cambridge: Cambridge University Press).

Wilding, P. (1982) *Professional Power and Social Welfare* (London: Routledge & Kegan Paul).

Wilding, P. (1992) 'The Public Sector in the 1980s', in Nick Manning and Robert Page (eds), *Social Policy Review* 4 (Canterbury: Social Policy Association).

Wilkinson, E. and Conze, E. (1934) *Why Fascism?* (London: Selwyn & Blount).

Williams, F. (1989) *Social Policy: A Critical Introduction* (Cambridge: Polity Press).

Williamson, B. (1990) *The Temper of the Times: British Society since World War II* (Oxford: Basil Blackwell).

Wilson, E. (1977) *Women and the Welfare State* (London: Tavistock).

Witz, A. (1992) *Professions and Patriarchy* (London: Routledge).

Wolfendon, J. (1978) *The Future of Voluntary Organisations* (London: Croom Helm).

Wooldridge, A. (1996) 'The English State and Educational Theory', in S. J. D. Green and R. C. Whiting (eds), *The Boundaries of the State in Modern Britain* (Cambridge: Cambridge University Press).

Wooton, B. (1959) 'Daddy Knows Best', *The Twentieth Century*, October, pp. 248–61.

Young, H. (1990) *One of Us* (London: Pan).

Young, K. (1985) 'Re-Reading the Municipal Progress: A Crisis Revisited', in Martin Loughlin M. D. Gelfand and K. Young (eds), *Half a Century of Municipal Decline* (London: George Allen & Unwin).

Zweiniger-Bargielowska, Ina (1994) 'Rationing, Austerity and the Conservative Party Recovery after 1945', *Historical Journal* 37(1), pp. 173–97.

INDEX